Classic
– AUSTRALIAN VERSE –

– Classic –
AUSTRALIAN
VERSE

Collected by Maggie Pinkney

The Five Mile Press

Contents

Introduction

AUSTRALIA was perceived by early European settlers as a bizarre place where the order of things was perversely topsy-turvy. In a bewildered tone, Richard Whately (1787-1863) wrote, 'Swans are not white but black as soot,' and went on to describe north winds that scorch and south winds that freeze – which must have seemed very strange to someone from the northern hemisphere. In his eccentric poem, 'The Kangaroo', Barron Field (1786-1846) went so far as to describe 'this fifth part of the earth' as an 'after-birth':

> *Not conceiv'd in the Beginning*
> *(For God bless'd His work at first,*
> *And saw that it was good),*
> *But emerg'd at the first sinning,*
> *And hence this barren wood!*

No doubt the convicts would have agreed with this view of their new, reluctantly adopted homeland.

Two Australian-born poets, Charles Harpur (1813-1868) and Henry Kendall (1839-1882) were among the first to write of the Australian landscape with any affection. Harpur's 'A Midsummer Noon in the Australian Bush' perfectly captures the bush's feeling of drowsiness and stillness, while Kendall's 'Bell-birds' hauntingly evokes the sights and sounds of the enchanting mountainside creeks and ferny glades of eastern Australia.

However, it was a later generation of poets whose verse helped to us to see our country clearly – in all its contrasting aspects – and gave us a sense of national identity.

At about the same time, the end of the nineteenth and early twentieth centuries, Australia's Heidelberg school of painters – Arthur Streeton, Tom Roberts, Frederick McCubbin, and others – were performing the same task in a different medium. They were the first artists to capture the unique 'Australian-ness' of the bush on canvas.

Foremost among the later generation of poets was the prolific A.B. ('Banjo') Paterson (1864-1941) who single-handedly provided us with most of our best-loved and most essentially Australian poems: 'The Man from Snowy River', 'Clancy of the Overflow', 'The Geebung Polo Club', and our unofficial national anthem 'Waltzing Matilda' – to name just a few. C.J. Dennis, Henry Lawson, Barcroft Boake, James Lister Cuthbertson, Louis Esson and Dorothea Mackellar were among the many other poets who helped to shape our growing national consciousness. The poems of Lawson (1867-1922), in particular, added to our appreci-ation of the Australian bush and her characters. Lawson also drew our attention to the special hardships faced by the women of the outback. Where Paterson's verse is uncompromisingly masculine, most of Lawson's poems have a softer, more feminine quality, often dealing with emotions rather than actions.

A cloak of anonymity covers another significant group of Australian versifiers: the authors of our many wonderful ballads and bush songs. First they described the plight of the convicts, and later the daring exploits of the bushrangers. Although the names of these poets are long forgotten their poignant verse s live on. 'The Wild Colonial Boy', 'Brave Ben Hall', 'The Kelly Gang' and 'Farewell to

Greta: A Ballad of Ned Kelly' are magnificent examples of this genre. They capture the excitement of the times and convey a sense of immediacy that no formal history could possibly achieve.

A delightfully vivid picture of a vanished Australia – peopled by rugged shearers, drovers, swaggies and poor selectors – emerges from this nostalgic anthology, as well as a deeper understanding of our colonial past.

The poems in this collection are a fitting commemoration of Australia's centenary of Federation.

Maggie Pinkney, 2001

Early Voices

There is a Place in Distant Seas

There is a place in distant seas
Full of contrarieties:
There, beasts have mallards' bills and legs,
Have spurs like cocks, like hens lay eggs.
There parrots walk upon the ground,
And grass upon the trees is found:
On other trees, another wonder!
Leaves without upper sides or under.
There pears you'll scarce with hatchet cut;
Stones are outside the cherry put;
Swans are not white, but black as soot.
There neither leaf, nor root, nor fruit
Will any Christian palate suit,
Unless in desperate need you'd fill ye
With root of fern and stalk of lily.
There missiles to far distance sent
Come whizzing back from whence they went;
There quadrupeds go on two feet;
There birds, although they cannot fly,
In swiftness with your greyhound vie.
With equal wonder you may see
The foxes fly from tree to tree;
And what they value most, so wary,
These foxes in their pockets carry.
There the voracious ewe-sheep crams
Her paunch with flesh of tender lambs,
Instead of beef, and bread, and broth,
Men feast on many a roasted moth.

The north winds scorch, but when the breeze is
Full from the south, why then it freezes;
The sun when you to face him turn ye,
From right to left performs his journey.
Now of what place could such strange tales
Be told with truth save New South Wales?

Richard Whately, 1787-1863

The Convicts' Rum Song

Cut yer name across me backbone,
  Stretch me skin across a drum,
Iron me up on Pinchgut Island
  From to-day till Kingdom Come!

I will eat yer Norfolk dumpling
  Like a juicy Spanish plum,
Even dance the Newgate Hornpipe
  If ye'll only give me rum!

Anonymous

Botany Bay

Farewell to old England forever,
Farewell to my rum-culls as well,
Farewell to the well-known Old Bailey
Where I used to cut such a swell.

Chorus:
Singing tooral-i-ooral-i-addity,
Singing tooral-i-ooral-i-ay,
Singing tooral-i-ooral-i-addity,
We're all bound for Botany Bay.

There's the captain as is our commander,
The bosun and all the ship's crew,
The first and the second class passengers
Knows what we poor convicts goes through.

It ain't leaving old England we cares about,
T'ain't cause we misspells what we knows,
It's just that us light-fingered gentry
Hops around with a log on our toes.

It's seven long years I've been serving,
And seven long more have to stay,
For bashing a cop in our alley,
And stealing his truncheon away.

Oh, if I had the wings of a turtle-dove
I'd soar on my pinions so high,
Slap-bang to the arms of my Polly-love,
And on her sweet bosom I'd die.

Now all you young dookies and duchesses,
Take warning from what I do say,
Mind all is your own as you toucheses
Or you'll join us in Botany Bay.

Traditional

The Lass in the Female Factory

The Currency Lads may fill their glasses,
And drink the health of the Currency Lasses,
But the lass I adore, the lass for me,
Is the lass in the Female Factory.

O! Molly's her name, and her name is Molly,
Although she was tried by the name of Polly;
She was tried and sent for death at Newry,
But the judge was bribed and so were the jury.

She got 'death recorded' in Newry town
For stealing her mistress's watch and gown;
Her little boy Paddy can tell you the tale,
His father was turnkey at Newry jail.

The first time I saw the comely lass
Was at Parramatta, going to Mass:
Says I 'I'll marry you now in an hour.'
Says she: 'Well, go and fetch Father Power.'

But I got in trouble that very same night!
Being drunk in the street I got in a fight:
A constable seized me – I gave him a box –
And was put in the watch-house and then in
  the stocks.

O! It's very unaisy as I remember
To sit in the stocks in the month of November,
With the north winds so hot, and the hot sun
  right over.
O! sure and it's no place at all for a lover!

'It's worse than the treadmill,' says I, 'Mr Dunn,
To sit here all day in the heat of the sun.'
'Either that or a dollar,' says he, 'for your folly' –
But if I had a dollar I'd drink it with Molly.

But now I am out again, early and late
I sigh and I cry at the Factory gate.
'O Mrs Reordon, late Mrs Farson,
O! won't you let Molly out very soon?'

'Is it Molly McGuigan,' says she to me.
'Is it now?' says I, for I know'd it was she.
'Is it her you mean that was put in the stocks
For beating her mistress, Mrs Cox?'

'O! yes and it is, madam, pray let me in.
I have brought her a half-pint of Cooper's best gin.
She likes it as well as she likes her own mother,
O! now let me in, madam, I am her brother.'

So the Currency Lads may fill their glasses,
And drink the health of the Currency Lasses,
But the lass I adore, the lass for me,
Is the lass in the Female Factory.

Anonymous

Jim Jones

O listen for a moment, and hear me tell my tale,
How o'er the sea from England I was compelled
  to sail.
The jury says, 'He's guilty,' and says the judge, says
  he,
'For life, Jim Jones, I'm sending you across the
  stormy sea.
'And take my tip before you ship to join the iron
  gang:
Don't get too gay at Botany Bay, or else you'll
  surely hang –
Or else you'll hang,' he says, says he, 'and after that,
  Jim Jones,
High up upon the gallows tree the crows will pick
  your bones.

'You'll have no time for mischief then, remember
  what I say:
They'll flog the poaching out of you, out there at
  Botany Bay.'

The waves were high upon the sea, the winds blew
  up in gales –
I would rather drown in misery than go to New
  South Wales.

The winds blew high upon the sea, and the pirates
  came along,
But the soldiers on our convict ship were full five
  hundred strong.
They opened fire and somehow drove that pirate
  ship away.
I'd rather have joined that pirate ship than come to
  Botany Bay.

For day and night the irons clang, and like poor
  galley-slaves
We toil and toil, and when we die must fill
  dishonoured graves.
But by and by I'll break my chain; into the bush
  I'll go,
And join the brave bushrangers there, Jack Donahue
  & Co.

And some dark night when everything is silent
  in the town
I'll kill the tyrants one and all, I'll shoot the floggers
  down:
I'll give the Law a little shock, remember what I say:
They'll yet regret they sent Jim Jones in chains to
  Botany Bay.

Traditional

Songs of the Squatters

The gum has no shade,
  And the wattle no fruit,
The parrots don't warble
  In trolls like the flute,
The cockatoo cooeth
  Not much like a dove
Yet fear not to ride
  To my station, my love;
Four hundred miles off
  Is goal of our way,
It is done in a week
  At but sixty a day;
The plains are all dusty;
  The creeks are all dried,
'Tis the fairest of weather
  To bring home my bride.
The blue vault of heaven
  Shall curtain thy form
One side of a gum tree
  The moonbeam must warm;
The whizzing mosquito
  Shall dance o'er thy head,
And the guana shall squat
  At the foot of thy bed;
The brave laughing jackass
  Shall sing thee to sleep,
And the snake o'er thy slumbers
  His vigils shall keep

Then sleep, lady, sleep,
  Without dreaming of pain,
Till the frost of the morning
  Shall wake thee again.
Our brave bridal bower
  I built not of stones.
Though, like old Doubting Castle,
  'Tis paved with bones,
The bones of sheep
  On whose flesh I have fed,
Where thy thin satin slipper
  Unshrinking may tread,
For the dogs have all polished
  Them clean with their teeth,
And they're better, believe me,
  Than what lies beneath.
My door has no hinge,
  And the window no pane,
They let out the smoke,
  But they let in the rain;
The frying pan serves us
  For table and dish,
And the tin pot of tea stands
  Still filled for your wish;
The sugar is brown,
  The milk is all done,
But the stick it is stirred with
  Is better than none.
The stockmen will swear,
  And the shepherds won't sing,

But a dog's a companion
  Enough for a king.
So fear not, fair lady,
  Your desolate way,
Your clothes will arrive
  In three months with my dray.
Then mount, lady, mount, to the wilderness fly,
My stores are laid in, and my shearing is nigh,
And our steeds, that through Sydney exultingly
wheel,
Must graze in a week on the banks of the Peel.

Robert Lowe, 1811-1892

The Kangaroo

Kangaroo, Kangaroo!
Thou spirit of Australia,
That redeems from utter failure,
From perfect desolation,
And warrants the creation
Of this fifth part of the Earth,
Which should seem an after-birth,
Not conceiv'd in the Beginning
(For God bless'd His work at first,
And saw that it was good),
But emerg'd at the first sinning,
When the ground was therefore curst;

And hence this barren wood!

Kangaroo, Kangaroo!
Tho' at first sight we should say,
In thy nature there may
Contradiction be involv'd,
It is quickly harmoniz'd.
Sphynx or mermaid realiz'd,
Or centaur unfabulous,
Would scarce be more prodigious,
Or Labrinthine Minotaur,
With which great Theseus did war,
Or Pegasus poetical.
Or hippogriff – chimera all!
But, what Nature would compile,
Nature knows how to reconcile;
And Wisdom, ever at her side,
Of all her children's justified.

She had made the squirrel fragile;
She had made the bounding hart;
But a third so strong and agile
Was beyond ev'n Nature's art.
So she join'd the former two
In thee, Kangaroo.

To describe thee, it is hard:
Converse of the camelopard,
Which beginneth camel-wise,
But endeth of the panther size,
Thy fore half, it would appear,

Had belong'd to some 'small deer'.
Such as liveth in a tree;
By the hinder, thou should'st be
A large animal of chase,
Bounding o'er the forest's space:
Join'd by some divine mistake,
None but Nature's hand can make –
Nature, in her wisdom's play,
On Creation's holiday.

For howso'er anomalous,
Thou yet are not incongruous,
Repugnant or preposterous,
Better-proportioned animal,
More graceful or ethereal,
Was never followed by the hound,
With fifty steps to thy one bound.
Thou can'st not be amended: no;
Be as thou art, thou best are so.

When sooty swans are once more rare,
And duck-moles the Museum's care,
Be still the glory of this land,
Happiest Work of finest Hand!

Barron Field, 1786-1846

Colonial Experience

When first I came to Sydney Cove
And up and down the streets did rove,
I thought such sights I ne'er did see
Since first I learnt my ABC.

Chorus:
Oh! it's broiling in the morning,
It's toiling in the morning,
It's broiling in the morning,
It's toiling all day long.

Into the park I took a stroll –
I felt just like a buttered roll.
A pretty name 'The Sunny South'
A better one 'The Land of Drouth!'

Next day into the bush I went,
On wild adventure I was bent,
Dame Nature's wonders I'd explore,
All thought of danger would ignore.

The mosquitoes and bull-dog ants
Assailed me even through my pants.
It nearly took my breath away
To hear the Jackass laugh so gay!

This lovely country, I've been told,
Abounds in silver and in gold.
You may pick it up all day,
Just as leaves in autumn lay!

Marines will chance this yarn believe,
But bluejackets you can't deceive,
Such pretty stories will not fit,
Nor can I their truth admit.

Some say there's lots of work to do,
Well, yes, but then, 'twixt me and you,
A man may toil and broil all day –
The big, fat man gets all the pay.

Mayhap such good things there may be,
But you may have them all, for me,
Instead of roaming foreign parts
I wish I'd studied the Fine Arts.

Anonymous

People and Places

A Midsummer Noon
in the Australian Bush

Not a sound disturbs the air,
There is quiet everywhere;
Over plains and over woods
What a mighty stillness broods!

All the birds and insects keep
Where the coolest shadows sleep;
Even the busy ants are found
Resting in their pebbled mound;
Even the locusts clingeth now
Silent to the barky bough;
Over hills and over plains
Quiet, vast and slumbrous, reigns.

Only there's a drowsy humming
From yon warm lagoon slow coming;
'Tis the dragon-hornet, see!
All bedaubed resplendently,
Yellow on a tawny ground –
Each rich spot nor square nor round,
Rudely heart-shaped, as it were
The blurred and hasty empress there
Of a vermael-crusted seal
Dusted o'er with golden meal.
Only there's a droning where
Yon bright beetle shines in air.
Tracks it in its gleaming flight
With a slanting beam of light,

Rising in the sunshine higher,
Till its shards flame out like fire.

Every other thing is still,
Save the ever-wakeful rill,
Whose cool murmur only throws
Cooler comfort round repose;
Or some ripple in the sea
Of leafy boughs, where lazily,
Tired summer, in her bower
Turning with the noontide hour,
Heaves a slumbrous breath ere she
Once more slumbers peacefully.

O 'tis easeful here to lie
Hidden from noon's scorching eye,
In this grassy cool recess
Musing thus of quietness.

Charles Harpur, 1813-1868

Solitude

Where the mocking lyrebird calls
To its mate among the falls
Of the mountain streams that play,
Each adown its tortuous way,
When the dewy-fingered even'
Veils the narrow'd glimpse of Heaven:
Where the morning re-illumes
Gullies full of ferny plumes,
And a woof of radiance weaves
Through high-hanging vaults of leaves;
There, 'mid giant turpentines,
Groups of climbing, clustering vines,
Rocks that stand like sentinels,
Guarding Nature's citadels;
Lowly flowering shrubs that grace
With their beauty all the place –
There I love to wander lonely,
With my dog companion only;
There indulge unworldly moods
In the mountain solitudes;
Far from all the gilded strife
Of our boasted 'social life',
Contemplating, spirit-free,
The majestic company
Grandly marching through the ages –
Heroes, martyrs, bards and sages –
They who bravely suffered long,
By their struggles waxing strong,

For the freedom of the mind,
For the rights of humankind!
Oh, for some awakening cause,
Where we face eternal laws,
Where we dare not turn aside,
Where the souls of men are tried –
Something of the nobler strife
Which consumes the dross of life,
To unite to truer aim,
To exalt to loftier fame!
Leave behind the bats and balls,
Leave the racers in the stalls,
Leave the cards forever shuffled,
Leave the yacht on seas unruffled,
Leave the haunts of pampered ease,
Leave your dull festivities! –
Better far the savage glen,
Fitter school for earnest men!

Henry Parkes, 1815-1896

Bell-birds

By channels of coolness the echoes are calling,
And down the dim gorges I hear the creek falling;
It lives in the mountains, where moss and the sedges
Touch with their beauty the banks and the ledges:
Through breaks of the cedar and sycamore bowers
Struggles the light that is love to the flowers.
And softer than slumber, and sweeter than singing,
The notes of the bell-birds are running and ringing.

The silver-voiced bell-birds, the darlings of daytime,
They sing in September the songs of the May-time.
When shadows wax strong, and the thunder-bolts
   hurtle,
They hide with their fear in the leaves of the myrtle;
When rain and the sunbeams shine mingled together,
They start up like fairies that follow fair weather,
And straightway the hues of the feathers unfolden
Are the green and the purple, the blue and the
   golden.

October, the maiden of bright yellow tresses,
Loiters for love in these cool wildernesses;
Loiters knee-deep in the grasses to listen,
Where dripping rocks gleam and the leafy pools
   glisten.
Then is the time when the water-moons splendid
Break with their gold, and are scattered or blended
Over the creeks, till the woodlands have warning
Of songs of the bell-bird and wings of the morning.

Welcome as water unkissed by the summers
Are the voices of bell-birds to thirsty far-comers.
When fiery December sets foot in the forest,
And the need of the wayfarer presses the sorest,
The bell-birds direct him to spring and to river,
With ring and with ripple, like runnels whose
  torrents
Are tossed by the pebbles and leaves in the currents.

Often I sit, looking back to a childhood
Mixt with the sight and the sounds of the wildwood,
Longing for power and sweetness of fashion
Lyrics with beats like heart-beats of passion –
Songs interwoven of lights and of laughters
Borrowed from bell-birds in far forest rafters;
So I might keep in the city and alleys
The beauty and strength of the deep mountain
  valleys,
Charming to slumber the pain of my losses
With glimpses of creeks and a vision of mosses.

Henry Kendall, 1839-1882

The Last of His Tribe

He crouches, and buries his face on his knees,
  And hides in the dark of his hair;
For he cannot look up to the storm-smitten trees,
  Or think of the loneliness there –
  Of the loss and the loneliness there.

The wallaroos grope through the tufts of the grass
  And turn to their coverts for fear;
But he sits in the ashes and lets them pass
  Where the boomerangs sleep with the spear –
  With the nullah, the sling and the spear.

Uloola, behold him! The thunder that breaks
  On the tops of the rocks with the rain,
And the wind which drives up with the salt of the lakes
  Have made him a hunter again –
  A hunter and fisher again.

For his eyes have been full with a smouldering
  thought;
  But he dreams of the hunts of yore,
And of foes that he sought, and of fights that he fought
  With those who will battle no more –
  Who will go to the battle no more.

It is well that the water which tumbles and fills
  Goes moaning and moaning along;
For an echo rolls out from the sides of the hills,
  And he starts at a wonderful song –

At the sound of a wonderful song.

And he sees, through the rents of the scattering fogs,
  The corroboree warlike and grim,
And the lubra who sat by the fire on the logs.
  To watch like a mourner for him –
  Like a mother and mourner for him.

Will he go in his sleep from these desolate lands,
  Like a chief, to the rest of his race,
With the honey-voiced woman who beckons and
  stands,
  And gleams like a dream in his face –
  Like a marvellous dream in his face?

Henry Kendall, 1839-1882

Are You the Cove?

'Are you the Cove?' he spoke the words
As swagmen only can;
The Squatter freezingly inquired,
'What do you mean, my man?'

'Are you the Cove?' his voice was stern,
His look was firm and keen;
Again the Squatter made reply,
'I don't know what you mean.'

'O! dash my rags! Let's have some sense –
You ain't a fool, by Jove,
Gammon you dunno what I mean:
I mean – are you the Cove?'

'Yes, I'm the Cove,' the Squatter said;
The Swagman answered, 'Right,
I thought as much: show me some place
Where I can doss tonight.'

'Tom Collins' (Joseph Furphy), 1843-1912

Tell Summer That I Died

When he was old and thin
And knew not night nor day,
He would sit up to say
Something of fire within.
How woefully his chin
Moved slowly as he tried
Some lusty words to say:
Tell Summer that I died.

When gladness sweeps the land,
And to the white sky
Cool butterflies go by,
And sheep in shadow stand;
When Love, the old command,
Turns every hate aside,
In the unstinted days
Tell Summer that I died.

John Shaw Neilson, 1872-1942

The Billy of Tea

You may talk of your whisky or talk of your beer,
I've something far better awaiting me here;
It stands on that fire beneath the gum-tree,
And you cannot lick it – a billy of tea.
So fill up your tumbler as high as you can,
You'll never persuade me it's not the best plan,
To let all the beer and the spirits go free
And stick to my darling old Billy of Tea.

I wake in the morning as soon as 'tis light,
And go to the nosebag to see it's all right,
That the ants on the sugar no mortgage have got,
And immediately sling my old billy-pot,
And while it's boiling the horses I seek,
And follow them down as far as the creek;
I take off the hobbles and let them go free,
And haste to tuck into my Billy of Tea.

And at night when I camp, if the day has been warm,
I give each of the horses their tucker of corn,
From the two in the pole to the one in the lead,
And the billy for each holds a comfortable feed;
Then the fire I start and the water I get,
And the corned beef and damper in order I set,
But I don't touch the grub, though so hungry I be,
I will wait till it's ready – the Billy of Tea.

Anonymous

The Bush

Give us from dawn to dark
  Blue of Australian skies,
Let there be none to mark
  Whither our pathway lies.

Give us when noontide comes
  Rest in the woodland free –
Fragrant breath of the gums,
  Cold, sweet scent of the sea.

Give us the wattle's gold
  And the dew-laden air,
And the loveliness bold
  Loneliest landscape wear.

These are the haunts we love,
  Glad with enchanted hours,
Bright as the heavens above,
  Fresh as the wild bush flowers.

James Lister Cuthbertson, 1851-1910

Where the Pelican Builds Her Nest

The horses were ready, the rails were down,
But the riders lingered still –
One had a parting word to say,
And one had his pipe to fill.
Then they mounted, one with a granted prayer,
And one with a grief unguessed.
'We are going,' they said as they rode away,
'Where the pelican builds her nest!'

They had told us of pastures wide and green,
To be sought past the sunset's glow;
Of rifts in the ranges by opal lit;
And gold 'neath the river's flow.
And thirst and hunger were banished words
When they spoke of that unknown West;
No drought they dreaded, no flood they feared,
Where the pelican builds her nest!

The creek at the ford was but fetlock deep
When we watched them crossing there;
The rains have replenished it thrice since then,
And thrice has the rock lain bare.
But the waters of Hope have flowed and fled,
And never from the blue hill's breast
Come back – by the sun and sands devoured –
Where the pelican builds her nest.

Mary Hannay Foott, 1846-1918

The Shearer's Wife

Before the glare o' dawn I rise
To milk the sleepy cows, an' shake
The droving dust from tired eyes,
Look round the rabbit traps, then bake
The children's bread.
There's hay to stook, an' beans to hoe,
An' ferns to cut i' th' scrub below;
Women must work, when men must go
Shearing from shed to shed.
I patch an' darn, now evening comes,
An' tired I am with labour sore,
Tired o' the bush, the cows, the gums,
Tired, but must dree for long months more
What no tongue tells.
The moon is lonely in the sky,
Lonely the bush, an' lonely I
Stare down the track no horse draws nigh
An' start at the cattle bells.

Louis Esson, 1879-1943

The Never-Never Land

By homestead, hut and shearing-shed,
  By railroad, coach and track –
By lonely graves where rest our dead,
  Up-Country and Out-back;
To where beneath the clustered stars
  The dreamy plains expand –
My home lies wide a thousand miles
  In the Never-Never Land.

It lies beyond the farming belt,
  Wide wastes of scrub and plain,
A blazing desert in the drought,
  A lake-land after rain;
To the skyline sweeps the waving grass,
  Or whirls the scorching sand –
A phantom land, a mystic realm!
  The Never-Never Land.

Where lone Mount Desolation lies,
  Mounts Dreadful and Despair –
'Tis lost beneath the rainless skies
  In hopeless deserts there.
It spreads nor'west by No-Man's Land –
  Where clouds are seldom seen –
To where the cattle stations lie
  Three hundred miles between.

The drovers of the Great Stock routes
  The strange Gulf country know –

Where, travelling from the southern droughts,
  The big lean bullocks go;
And camped by night where plains lie wide,
  Like some old ocean's bed,
The watchmen in the starlight ride
  Round fifteen hundred head.

Lest in the city I forget
  True mateship after all,
My water-bag and billy yet
  Are hanging on the wall;
And I, to save my soul again,
  Would tramp to sunsets grand
With sad-eyed mates across the plain
  In the Never-Never Land.

Henry Lawson, 1867-1922

The Camp Fire

Reclining near his golden fire,
Alone within the silent bush,
He slowly smokes his evening briar,
And listens to the hovering hush.

The flames are points of falchion-blades,
Light-giving in their wheel and dance;
They gild the underleaf that fades
Above into a glooming trance.

The boles around rise to the night,
Ashen and grey, in solemn-wise,
Opening a heaven of starry light,
Dark violet-blue of nameless dyes.

Thoughts, many as the leaves in the woods
Touched by the first autumnal cold,
That fall and lie, in drifting floods,
Draw home with legendary gold.

Fanned from the fire a burning brand
Lights the bronzed glade with vivid glow;
On earth he whispering lays his hand:
'Mother, to thy calm rest I go.'

Barcroft Boake, 1866-1892

Clancy of the Overflow

I had written him a letter which I had, for want
of better
Knowledge, sent to where I met him down the
Lachlan years ago;
He was shearing when I knew him, so I sent the
letter to him,
Just on spec, addressed as follows, 'Clancy of the
Overflow'.

And answer came directed in a writing unexpected
(And I think the same was written with a thumb-nail
dipped in tar):
'Twas his shearing mate who wrote it, and verbatim
I will quote it:
'Clancy's gone to Queensland droving, and we don't
know where he are.'

In my wild erratic fancy visions come to me of
Clancy
Gone a-droving 'down the Cooper' where the
Western drovers go;
As the stock are slowly stringing, Clancy rides behind
them singing,
For the drover's life has pleasures that the townsfolk
never know.

And the bush has friends to meet him, and their
kindly voices greet him
In the murmur of the breezes and the river on its bars

And he sees the vision splendid of the sunlit plains
    extended,
And at night the wondrous glory of the everlasting
    stars.

I am sitting in my dingy little office, where a stingy
Ray of sunlight struggles feebly down between the
    houses tall,
And the foetid air and gritty of the dusty, dirty city,
Through the open window floating, spreads its
    foulness over all.

And in place of lowing cattle, I can hear the
    fiendish rattle
Of the tramways and the buses making hurry down
    the street;
And the language uninviting of the gutter children
    fighting
Comes fitfully and faintly through the ceaseless
    tramp of feet.

And the hurrying people daunt me, and their pallid
    faces haunt me
As they shoulder one another in their rush and
    nervous haste,
With the eager eyes and greedy, and their stunted
    forms and weedy,
For the townsfolk have no time to grow, they have
    no time to waste.

And I somehow rather fancy that I'd like to change
    with Clancy.

Like to take a turn at droving where the seasons
  come and go,
While he faced the round eternal of the cash-book
  and the journal –
But I doubt he'd suit the office, Clancy of the
  Overflow.

A.B. ('Banjo') Paterson, 1864-1941

The Blue Mountains

Above the ashes straight and tall,
  Through ferns with moisture dripping,
I climb beneath the sandstone wall,
  My feet on mosses slipping.

Like ramparts round the valley's edge
  The tinted cliffs are standing.
With many a broken wall and ledge,
  And many a rocky landing.

And round about their rugged feet
  Deep ferny dells are hidden
In shadowed depths, whence dust and heat
  Are banished and forbidden.

The stream that, crooning to itself,
  Comes down a tireless rover,
Flows calmly to the rocky shelf,

And there leaps bravely over.

Now pouring down, now lost in spray
  When mountain breezes sally,
The water strikes the rock midway,
  And leaps into the valley.

Now in the west the colours change,
  The blue with crimson blending;
Behind the far Dividing Range,
  The sun is fast descending.

And mellowed day comes o'er the place,
  And softens ragged edges;
The rising moon's great placid face
Looks gravely o'er the ledges.

Henry Lawson, 1867-1922

Echoes of Wheels...

Echoes of wheels and singing lashes
  Wake on the morning air;
Out of the kitchen a youngster dashes,
  Giving the ducks a scare.
Three jiffs from house to gully,
  And over the bridge to the gate;
And then a panting little boy
  Climbs on the rails to wait.

For there is long-whipped cursing Bill
　With four enormous logs,
Behind a team with the white-nosed leader's
　Feet in the sucking bogs.
Oh it was grand to see them stuck
　And grand to see them strain,
Until the magical language of Bill
　Had got them out again!

I foxed them to the shoulder turn,
　I saw him work them round,
And die into the secret bush,
　Leaving only sound.

And it isn't bullocks I recall,
　Nor waggons my memory sees;
But in the scented bush a track
　Turning among the trees.

Oh track where the brown leaves fall
　In dust to our very knees!

And it isn't the wattle that I recall,
Nor the sound of the bullocky's singing lash,
When the cloven hoofs in the puddles splash;
But the rumble on an unseen load
Swallowed along the hidden road
　Turning among the trees!

'Furnely Maurice' (Frank Wilmot), 1881-1942

The Women of the West

They left the vine-wreathed cottage and the mansion
on the Hill,
The houses in the busy streets where life is never
still,
The pleasures of the city, and the friends they
cherished best,
For love they faced the wilderness – the Women of
the West.

The roar and rush and fever of the city died away,
And old-time joys and faces – they were gone for
many a day;
In their place the lurching coach-wheel, or the
creaking bullock chains;
Or the everlasting sameness of the never-ending
plains.

In the slab-built, zinc-roofed homestead of some
lately-taken run,
In the tent beside the 'bankment of a railway just
begun,
In the huts on new selections, in the camps of man's
unrest,
On the frontiers of the Nation, live the Women of
the West.

The red sun robs their beauty, and, in weariness
and pain,
The slow years steal the nameless grace that never
comes again;
And there are hours men cannot soothe, and words

men cannot say –
The nearest woman's face may be a hundred miles
away.

The wide Bush holds the secrets of their longings
and desires,
When the white stars in reverence light their holy
altar-fires,
And silence, like the touch of God, sinks deep into
the breast –
Perchance He hears and understands the Women of
the West.

For them no trumpet sounds the call, no poet plies
his arts –
They only hear the beating of their gallant, loving
hearts,
But they have sung with silent lives the song all
songs above –
The holiness, the sacrifice, the dignity of love.

Well have we held our fathers' creed. No call has
passed us by.
We faced and fought the wilderness, we sent our
sons to die.
And we have hearts to do and dare, and yet, o'er
all the rest,
The hearts that made the Nation were the Women of
the West.

George Essex Evans, 1863-1909

Hay, Hell and Booligal

'You come and see me, boys,' he said;
'You'll find a welcome and a bed
And whisky any time you call;
Although our township hasn't got
The name of quite a lively spot –
You see, I live in Booligal.

'And people have an awful down
Upon the district and the town –
Which worse than Hell itself they call;
In fact, the saying far and wide
Along the Riverina side
Is 'Hay and Hell and Booligal'.

'No doubt it suits 'em very well
To say it's worse than Hay or Hell,
But don't you heed their talk at all;
Of course, there's heat – no one denies –
And sand and dust and stacks of flies,
And rabbits, too, at Booligal.

'But such a pleasant, quiet place,
You never see a stranger's face –
They hardly ever care to call;
The drovers mostly pass it by;
They reckon that they'd rather die
Than spend a night in Booligal.

'The big mosquitoes frighten some –
You'll lie awake to hear 'em hum –
And snakes about the township crawl;

But shearers, when they get their cheque,
They never come along and wreck
The blessed town of Booligal.

'But down in Hay the shearers come
And fill themselves with fighting rum,
And chase blue devils up the wall,
And fight the snaggers every day,
Until there is a deuce to pay –
There's none of that in Booligal.

'Of course, there isn't much to see –
The billiard table used to be
The great attraction for us all,
Until some careless, drunken curs
Got sleeping on it in their spurs,
And ruined it, in Booligal.

'Just now there is a howling drought
That pretty near has starved us out –
It never seems to rain at all;
But if there should come any rain,
You couldn't cross the black soil plain –
You'd have to stop in Booligal.'

'We'd have to stop!' With bated breath
We pray that both in life and death
Our fate in other lines might fall:
'Oh, send us to our just reward
In Hay or Hell, but, gracious Lord,
Deliver us from Booligal!'

A.B. ('Banjo') Paterson, 1864-1941

Bullocky Bill

As I came down Talbingo Hill
I heard a maiden cry,
'There goes old Bill the Bullocky –
He's bound for Gundagai.'

A better poor old beggar
Never cracked an honest crust,
A tougher poor old beggar
Never drug a whip through dust.

His team got bogged on the Five-Mile Creek,
Bill lashed and swore, and cried,
'If Nobbie don't get me out of this
I'll tattoo his bloody hide.'

But Nobbie strained and broke the yoke
And poked out the leader's eye,
And the dog sat on the tucker-box
Five miles from Gundagai.

Traditional

The Song of Australia

There is a land where summer skies
Are gleaming with a thousand dyes,
Blending in witching harmonies,
In harmonies.
And grassy knoll and forest height
Are flushing in the rosy light,
And all above is azure bright,
Australia, Australia, Australia.

There is a land where honey flows,
Where laughing corn luxuriant grows,
Land of the myrtle and the rose,
Land of the rose.
On hill and plain the clustering vine
Is gushing out with purple wine,
And cups are quaffed to thee and thine,
Australia, Australia, Australia.

There is a land where treasures shine
Deep in the dark unfathomed mine,
For worshippers at Mammon's shrine,
At Mammon's shrine.
Where gold lies hid, and rubies gleam,
And fabled wealth no more doth seem
The idle fancy of a dream,
Australia, Australia, Australia.

There is a land where homesteads peep
From sunny plain and woodland steep.

And love and joy bright vigils keep,
Bright vigils keep.
Where the glad voice of childish glee
Is mingled with the melody
Of nature's hidden minstrelsy,
Australia, Australia, Australia.

There is a land where floating free,
From mountain top to girdling sea.
A proud flag waves exultingly,
Exultingly.
And Freedom's sons the banner bear,
No shackled slave can breathe the air,
Fairest of Britain's daughters fair,
Australia, Australia, Australia.

Caroline Carleton, 1820-1874

Bill Brown

I met Bill Brown on Prospect Track
Astride a camel cow;
An' I said, 'I heard you had the sack,
An' where are you heading now?'

'Well, mate,' said William, 'I thought it out,
An' I sez to myself, sez I:
There's not much hope for the rouseabout,
As the rousy can testify.

'So I'll drink the honey of Freedom's Cup,
An' do as it pleases Brown;
I'll roll me swag when the sun gets up,
An' I'll camp when the sun goes down.

'I'm makin' out where the diggers go,
Where the reefs run deep an' wide;
I'll wet my whistle at Tally-ho,
An' I'll yard me a Western bride.

'She'll make me rugs with skins I get
When I'm off o' the veins of gold;
She'll strip an' thatch when the days are wet,
An' she'll stoke when the nights are cold.

'With only a fire in the trackless zone,
She'll cook like a chef, bet you;
Whatever she needs she will find alone
For her salmagundi too.

'If the tracks are barren this moke I've got
Will do with a mulga-tree,
An' the hobble-chains an' the old quart-pot
Still jangle a tune to me.'

He filled his pipe ere he said, 'So long!'
An' he rode where the sun grows red;
Where the bold are lured with a golden song
At times to a dead man's bed.

Though many ask, 'tis a nut to crack,
Where old Bill Brown is now;

He was heard of last on the Prospect Track
Astride of a camel cow.

Edward S. Sorenson, 1869-1939

My Country

The love of field and coppice,
Of green and shaded lanes,
Of ordered woods and gardens
Is running in your veins.
Strong love of grey-blue distance,
Brown streams and soft, dim skies –
I know but cannot share it,
My love is otherwise.

I love a sunburnt country,
A land of sweeping plains,
Of ragged mountain ranges,
Of droughts and flooding rains,
I love her far horizons,
I love her jewel-sea,
Her beauty and her terror –
The wide brown land for me!

The stark white ring-barked forests,
All tragic to the moon,
The sapphire-misted mountains,
The hot gold hush of noon,

Green tangle of the brushes
Where lithe lianas coil
And orchids deck the tree-tops,
And ferns the warm dark soil.

Core of my heart, my country!
Her pitiless blue sky,
When, sick at heart, around us
We see the cattle die –
But then the grey clouds gather,
And we can bless again
The drumming of an army,
The steady soaking rain.

Core of my heart, my country!
Land of the rainbow gold,
For flood and fire and famine
She pays us back threefold.
Over the thirsty paddocks,
Watch, after many days,
The filmy veil of greenness
That thickens as we gaze ...

An opal-hearted country,
A wilful, lavish land –
All you who have not loved her,
 You will not understand –
Though Earth holds many splendours,
Wherever I may die,
I know to what brown country
My homing thoughts will fly.

Dorothea Mackellar, 1885-1968

The Digger's Song

Scrape the bottom of the hole; gather up the stuff!
Fossick in the crannies, lest you leave a grain behind!
Just another shovelful and that'll be enough –
Now we'll take it to the bank and see what we can
  find …
Give the dish a twirl around!
Let the water swirl around!
Gently let it circulate – there's music in the swish
And the tinkle of the gravel
As the pebbles quickly travel
Around in merry circles on the bottom of the dish.

Ah, if man could wash his life – if he only could!
Panning off the evil deeds, keeping but the good:
What a mighty lot of diggers' dishes would be sold!
Though I fear the heap of tailings would be greater
  than the gold …
Give the dish a twirl around!
Let the water swirl around!
Man's the sport of circumstances however he may
  wish.
Fortune, are you there now?
Answer to my prayer now –
Drop a half-ounce nugget in the bottom of the dish.

Gently let the water lap! Keep the corners dry!
That's about the place the gold will generally stay.
What was the bright particle that just then caught
  my eye?

I fear me by the look of things 'twas only yellow
   clay ...
Just another twirl around!
Let the water swirl around!
That's the way we rob the river of its golden fish ...
What's that ... Can't we snare one?
Bah! There's not a colour in the bottom of the dish.

Barcroft Boake, 1866-1892

Australia's on the Wallaby

Our fathers came to search for gold,
The mine has proved a duffer;
From bankers, boss and syndicate
We always had to suffer ...
They fought for freedom for themselves,
Themselves and mates to toil,
But Australia's sons are weary
And the billy's on the boil.

Australia's on the wallaby,
Just listen to the coo-ee;
For the kangaroo, he rolls his swag
And the emu shoulders bluey.
The boomerangs are whizzing round,
The dingo scratches gravel;
The possum, bear and bandicoot
Are all upon the travel.

The cuckoo calls the bats and now
The pigeon and the shag
The mallee-hen and platypus
Are rolling up their swag;
For the curlew sings a sad farewell
Beside the long lagoon,
And the brolga does his last-way waltz
To the lyrebird's mocking tune.

There's tiger-snakes and damper, boys,
And what's that on the coals?
There's droughts and floods and ragged duds
And dried-up waterholes;
There's shadeless trees and sun-scorched plains,
All asking us to toil;
But Australia's sons are weary
And the billy's on the boil.

Anonymous

The Roaring Days

The night too quickly passes
  And we are growing old,
So let us fill our glasses
  And toast the Days of Gold;
When finds of wondrous treasure
  Set all the South ablaze,
And you and I were faithful mates

All through the Roaring Days.

Then stately ships came sailing
  From every harbour's mouth,
And sought the Land of Promise
  That beaconed in the South;
Then southward streamed their streamers
  And swelled their canvas full
To speed the wildest dreamers
  E'er borne in vessel's hull.

Their shining Eldorado
  Beneath the southern skies
Was day and night for ever
  Before their eager eyes.
The brooding bush awakened,
  Was stirred in wild unrest,
And all the year a human stream
  Went pouring to the West.

The rough bush roads re-echoed
  The bar-room's noisy din,
When troops of stalwart horsemen
  Dismounted at the inn.
And oft the hearty greetings
  And hearty clasp of hands
Would tell of sudden meetings
  Of friends from other lands.

And when the cheery camp-fire
  Explored the bush with gleams,
The camping-grounds were crowded

With caravans of teams;
Then home the jests were driven
  And good old songs were sung,
And choruses were given
  The strength of heart and lung.

Oft when the camps were dreaming,
  And fires began to pale,
Through rugged ranges gleaming
  Swept on the Royal Mail.
Behind six foaming horses,
  And lit by flashing lamps,
Old Cobb and Co., in royal state,
  Went dashing past the camps.

Oh, who would paint a goldfield,
  And paint the picture right,
As old Adventure saw it
  In early morning's light?
The yellow mounds of mullock
  With spots of red and white,
The scattered quartz that glistened
  Like diamonds in light;

The azure line of ridges,
  The bush of darkest green,
The little homes of calico
  That dotted all the scene.
The flat straw hats, with ribands,
  That old engravings show –
The dress that still reminds us

Of sailors long ago.

I hear the fall of timber
  From distant flats and fells,
The pealing of the anvils
  As clear as little bells,
The rattle of the cradle,
  The clack of windlass boles,
The flutter of the crimson flags
  Above the golden holes.

Ah, then their hearts were bolder,
  And if Dame Fortune frowned
Their swags they'd lightly shoulder
  And tramp to other ground.
Oh, they were lion-hearted
  Who gave our country birth!
Stout sons, of stoutest fathers born,
  From all the lands on earth!

Those golden days are vanished,
  And altered is the scene;
The diggings are deserted,
  The camping-grounds are green;
The flaunting flag of progress
  Is in the West unfurled,
The mighty Bush with iron rails
  Is tethered to the world.

Henry Lawson, 1867-1922

At the Melting of the Snow

There's a sunny Southern Land,
And it's there that I would be
Where the big hills stand
In the South Countrie!
When the wattles bloom again,
Then it's time for us to go
To the old Monaro country
At the melting of the snow.

To the East or to the West,
Or wherever you may be,
You will find no place
Like the South Countrie.
For the skies are blue above,
And the grass is green below,
In the old Monaro country
At the melting of the snow.

Now the team is in the plough,
And the thrushes start to sing,
And the pigeons on the bough
Are rejoicing at the Spring.
So come my comrades all,
Let us saddle up and go
To the old Monaro country
At the melting of the snow.

A.B.('Banjo') Paterson, 1864-1941

A Bush Girl

She's milking in the rain and dark,
  As did her mother in the past.
The wretched shed of poles and bark,
  Rent by the wind, is leaking fast.
She sees the 'home-roof' black and low,
  Where, balefully, the hut-fire gleams –
And, like her mother, long ago,
  She has her dreams; she has her dreams.

The daybreak haunts the dreary scene,
  The brooding ridge, the blue-grey bush,
The 'yard' where all her years have been
  Is ankle-deep in dung and slush;
She shivers as the hours drag on,
  Her threadbare dress of sackcloth seems;
But, like her mother, years agone,
  She has her dreams; she has her dreams.

The sullen 'breakfast' where they cut
  The blackened 'junk'. The lowering face,
As though a crime were in the hut,
  As though a curse were on the place;
The muttered question and reply,
  The tread that shakes the rotting beams,
The nagging mother, thin and dry –
  God help the girl! She has her dreams.

Then for 'th' separator' start
  Most wretched hour in all her life,

With 'horse' and harness, dress and cart,
  No Chinaman would give his wife;
Her heart is sick for light and love,
  Her face is often fair and sweet,
And her intelligence above
  The minds of all she's like to meet.

She reads, by slush-lamp, maybe,
  When she has dragged her weary round,
And dreams of cities by the sea
  (Where butter's up, so much the pound),
Of different men from those she knows,
  Of shining tides and broad bright streams;
Of theatres and city shows,
  And her release! She has her dreams.

Could I gain her a little rest,
  A little light, if but for one,
I think that it would be the best
  Of any good I may have done.
But, after all, the paths we go
  Are not so glorious as they seem,
And – if 'twill help her heart to know –
  I've had my dream. 'Twas but a dream.

Henry Lawson, 1867-1922

The Traveller

As I rode into Burrumbeet,
I met a man with funny feet;
And, when I paused to ask him why
His feet were strange, he rolled his eye
And said the rain would spoil the wheat;
So I rode on to Burrumbeet.

As I rode into Beetaloo
I met a man whose nose was blue;
And when I asked him how he got
A nose like that, he answered, 'What
Do bullocks mean when they say "Moo"?'
So I rode on to Beetaloo.

As I rode into Ballarat,
I met a man who wore no hat:
And, when I said he might take cold,
He cried 'The hills are quite as old
As yonder plains, but not so flat.'
So I rode on to Ballarat.

As I rode into Gundagai,
I met a man and passed him by
Without a nod, without a word.
He turned, and said he'd never heard
Or seen a man so wise as I,
But I rode on to Gundagai.

As I rode homeward, full of doubt,
I met a stranger riding out;

A foolish man he seemed to me;
But 'Nay, I am yourself,' said he.
'Just as you were when you rode out,'
So I rode homeward, free of doubt.

C.J. Dennis, 1876-1938

Where the Dead Men Lie

On the wastes of the Never Never –
  That's where the dead men lie!
There where the heat-waves dance forever –
  That's where the dead men lie!
That's where the Earth's loved sons are keeping
Endless Tryst; not the west wind sweeping
Feverish pinions can wake the sleeping
  Out where the dead men lie!

Where brown Summer and Death have mated –
  That's where the dead men lie!
Loving with fiery lust unsated –
  That's where the dead men lie
Out where the grinning skulls bleach whitely
Under the saltbush sparkling brightly,
Out where the wild dogs chorus nightly –
  That's where the dead men lie ...!

Deep in the yellow, flowing river –
  That's where the dead men lie!

Under the banks where the shadows quiver –
  That's where the dead men lie!
Where the platypus twists and doubles,
Leaving a train of tiny bubbles;
Rid at last of their earthly troubles –
  That's where the dead men lie!

East and backward faces turning –
  That's how the dead men lie!
Gaunt arms stretched with a violent yearning –
  That's how the dead men lie!
Oft in the fragrant hush of nooning
Hearing again their mother's crooning,
Wrapt for aye in a dreamful swooning –
  That's where the dead men lie!

Only the hand of Night can free them –
  That's when the dead men fly!
Only the frightened cattle see them –
  See the dead go by!
Cloven hoofs beating out one measure,
Bidding the stockmen know no leisure –
That's when the dead men take their pleasure!
  That's when the dead men fly!

Ask, too, the never-sleeping drover:
  He sees the dead pass by;
Hearing them call to their friends – the plover,
  Hearing the dead men cry;
Seeing their faces stealing, stealing,
Hearing their laughter, pealing, pealing,

Watching their grey forms wheeling, wheeling
  Round where the cattle lie!

Strangled by thirst and fierce privation –
  That's how the dead men die!
Out on Moneygrub's farthest station –
  That's how the dead men die!
Hard-faced grey-beards, youngsters callow;
Some mounds cared for, some left fallow;
Some deep down, yet others shallow:
  Some having but the sky.

Moneygrub, he sips his claret,
  Looks with complacent eye
Down at his watch-chain, eighteen carat –
  There, in his club, hard by:
Recks not that every link is stamped with
Names of men whose limbs are cramped with
Too long lying in grave-mould, camped with
  Death where the dead men lie.

Barcroft Boake, 1866-1892

Shearers

No church-bell rings them from the Track
    No pulpit lights their blindness –
Tis hardship, drought, and homelessness
    That teach those Bushmen kindness:
The mateship born, in barren lands,
    Of toil and thirst and danger,
The camp-fare for the wanderer set,
    The first place to the stranger.

They do the best they can today –
    Take no thought of the morrow:
Their way is not the old-world way –
    They live to lend and borrow.
When shearing's done and cheques gone wrong,
    They call it 'time to slither!' –
They saddle up and say 'So-long!'
    And ride the Lord knows whither.

And though he may be brown or black,
    Or wrong man there, or right man,
The mate that's steadfast to his mates
    They call that man a 'white man!'
They tramp in mateship side by side –
    The Protestant and Roman –
They call no biped lord or sir,
    And touch their hat to no man.

They carry in their swags, perhaps,
    A portrait and a letter –

And, maybe, deep down in their hearts,
  The hope of 'something better'.
Where lonely miles are long to ride,
  And long, hot days recurrent,
There's lots of time to think of men
  They might have been – but weren't.

They turn their faces to the west
  And leave the world behind them
(Their drought-dry graves are seldom set
  Where even mates can find them.)
They know too little of the world
  To rise to wealth and greatness:
But in these lines I gladly pay
  My tribute to their straightness.

Henry Lawson (1867-1922)

Condamine Bells

By a forge near a hut on the Condamine River
  A blacksmith laboured at his ancient trade;
With his hammer swinging and his anvil ringing
  He fashioned bells from a crosscut blade.

And while he toiled by the Condamine River
  He sang a song for a job well done:
And the song and the clamour of his busy hammer
  Merged and mingled in a tempered tone.

And his bell rang clear from the Condamine River
  To the Gulf, to the Leeuwin, over soil and sand;
Desert eagles winging heard his stock-bells ringing
  As a first voice singing in a songless land.

The smith is lost to the Condamine River,
  Gone is the humpy where he used to dwell;
But the songs and the clamour of his busy hammer
  Ring on through the land in the Condamine Bell.

Jack Sorensen, 1907-1949

Country Fellows

When country fellows come to town,
And meet to have a chat,
They bring the news from Camperdown,
Birchip and Ballarat.
Wisely they talk of wheat and wool
From Boort and Buningyong,
From Warragul and Warrnambool,
From Junee and Geelong.

Ted tells them how the crops are now
Well up round Bullarook,
And Fred describes the champion cow
He bred at Quambatook.
'If rain comes soon 'twill be a boon,'
Says Clive of Koo-wee-rup.
'Too right,' says Nick of Nar-nar-goon;
'The grass wants fetchin' up.'

And I who have been country bred,
And love the country still,
I listen wistfully to Ted
And George and Joe and Bill.
I see again the peaceful scene,
I hear them talk of paddocks green,
At Yea and Crogan's Dam,
Koroit, Kerang and Moulamein;
Then, dreaming of the might-have-been,
I go home in a tram.

C.J. Dennis, 1876-1938

Andy's Gone with Cattle

Our Andy's gone with cattle now –
  Our hearts are out of order –
With drought he's gone to battle now
  Across the Queensland border.

He's left us in dejection now,
  Our thoughts with him are roving:
It's dull on this selection now;
  Since Andy went a-droving.

Who now shall wear the cheerful face
  In times when things are slackest?
And who shall whistle round the place
  When Fortune frowns her blackest?

Oh, who shall cheek the squatter now
  When he comes round us snarling?
His tongue is growing hotter now
  Since Andy crossed the Darling.

Oh, may the showers in torrents fall,
  And all the tanks run over;
And may the grass grow green and tall
  In pathways of the drover ...

And may good angels send the rain
  On desert stretches sandy:
And when the summer comes again
  God grant 'twill bring us Andy.

Henry Lawson, 1867-1922

Andy's Return

With pannikins all rusty,
  And billy burnt and black,
And clothes all torn and dusty,
  That scarcely hide his back;
With sun-cracked saddle-leather,
  And knotted greenhide rein,
And face burnt brown with weather,
  Our Andy's home again!

His unkempt hair is faded
  With sleeping in the wet,
He's looking old and jaded;
  But he is hearty yet.
With eyes sunk in their sockets –
  But merry as of yore;
With big cheques in his pockets,
  Our Andy's home once more!

Old Uncle's bright and cheerful;
  He wears a smiling face;
And Aunty's never tearful
  Now Andy's round the place.
Old Blucher barks for gladness;
  He broke his rusty chain,
And leapt in joyous madness
  When Andy came again.

With tales of flood and famine,
  On distant northern tracks,

And shady yarns – 'baal gammon!'
  Of dealings with the blacks,
From where the skies hang lazy
  On many a northern plain,
From regions dim and hazy
  Our Andy's home again!

His toil is nearly over;
  He'll soon enjoy his gains,
Not long he'll be a drover,
  And cross the lonely plains.
We'll happy be for ever
  When he'll no longer roam
But by some deep, cool river
  Will make us all a home.

Henry Lawson, 1867-1922

The Pannikin Poet

There's nothing here sublime,
But just a roving rhyme,
Run off to pass the time,
With naught titanic in
The theme that it supports
And, though it treats of quarts,
It's bare of golden thoughts –
It's just a pannikin.

I think it's rather hard
That each Australian bard –
Each wan poetic card –
With thoughts galvanic in
His fiery soul alight,
In wild aerial flight,
Will sit him down and write
About a pannikin.

He makes some new chum fare
From out his English lair
To hunt the native bear,
That curious mannikin;
And then when times get bad
That wand'ring English lad
Writes out a message sad
Upon his pannikin:
'Oh, mother, think of me
Beneath the wattle tree.'
(For you bet that he
Will drag the wattle in.)
'Oh, mother, here I think
That I shall have to sink
There ain't a single drink
The water bottle in.'

The dingo homeward hies
The sooty crows uprise
And caw their fierce surprise
A tone Satanic in;
And bearded bushmen tread

Around the sleeper's head –
'See here – the bloke is dead.
Now, where's his pannikin?'

They read his words and weep,
And lay him down to sleep
Where wattle branches sweep
A style mechanic in;
And, reader, that's the way
The poets of today
Spin out their little lay
About a pannikin.

A.B. ('Banjo') Paterson, 1864-1941

Middleton's Rouseabout

Tall and freckled and sandy,
　Face of a country lout;
This was the picture of Andy,
　Middleton's rouseabout.

Type of a coming nation,
　In the land of cattle and sheep,
Worked on Middleton's station,
　'Pound a week and his keep.'

On Middleton's wide dominions
　Plied the stockwhip and shears;

Hadn't any opinions,
  Hadn't any 'idears'.

Swiftly the years went over,
  Liquor and drought prevailed;
Middleton went as a drover
  After his station had failed.

Type of a careless nation,
  Men who are soon played out,
Middleton was – and his station
  Was bought by the Rouseabout.

Flourishing beard and sandy,
  Tall and solid stout;
This is the picture of Andy,
  Middleton's Rouseabout.

Now on his own dominions
  Works with his overseers:
Hasn't any opinions,
  Hasn't any idears.

Henry Lawson, 1867-1922

To a Billy

Old billy – battered, brown and black
With many days of camping,
Companion of the bulging sack,
And friend in all our tramping;
How often on the Friday night –
Your cubic measure testing –
With jam and tea we stuffed you tight
Before we started nesting!

How often in the moonlight pale,
Through gums and gullies toiling,
We've been the first the hill to scale,
The first to watch you boiling;
When at the lane the tent was spread
The silver wattle under,
And early shafts of rosy red
Cleft sea-borne mists asunder!

And so, old Billy, you recall
A host of sunburnt faces,
And bring us back again to all
The best of camping places.
True flavour of the bush you bear
Of camp and its surrounding.
Of freedom and of open air,
Of healthy life abounding

James Lister Cuthbertson, 1851-1910

How M'Ginnis Went Missing

Let us ease our idle chatter,
Let the tears bedew our cheek,
For the man from Tallangatta
Has been missing for a week.

Where the roaring, flooded Murray
Covered all the lower land,
There he started in a hurry,
With a bottle in his hand.

And his fate is hid forever,
But the public seem to think
That he slumbered by the river,
'Neath the influence of drink.

And they scarcely seem to wonder
That the river, wide and deep,
Never woke him with its thunder,
Never stirred him in his sleep.

As the crushing logs came sweeping,
And their tumult filled the air,
Then M'Ginnis murmured, sleeping,
''Tis a wake to ould Kildare.'

So the river rose and found him
Sleeping softly by the stream,
And the cruel waters drowned him
Ere he wakened from his dream.

And the blossom-tufted wattle,
Blooming brightly on the lea
Saw M'Ginnis and the bottle
Going drifting out to sea.

A.B. ('Banjo) Paterson, 1864-1941

The Drover's Sweetheart

An hour before the sun goes down
　Behind the ragged boughs,
I go across the little run
　To bring the dusty cows;
And once I used to sit and rest
　Beneath the fading dome,
For there was one that I loved best
　Who'd bring the cattle home.

Our yard is fixed with double bails;
　Round one the grass is green,
The Bush is growing through the rails,
　The spike is rusted in:
It was from there his freckled face
　Would turn and smile at me,
For he'd milk seven in the race
　While I was milking three.

He kissed me twice and once again
　And rode across the hill;
The pint-pots and the hobble-chain —
　I hear them jingling still.

About the hut as sunlight fails
  The fire shines through the cracks –
I climb the broken stockyard rails
  And watch the bridle-tracks.

And he is coming home again –
  He wrote from Evatt's Rock;
A flood was in the Darling then
  And foot-rot in the flock.
The sheep were falling thick and fast
  A hundred miles from town,
And when he reached the line at last
  He trucked the remnant down.

And so he'll have to stand the cost;
  His luck was always bad,
Instead of making more, he lost
  The money that he had;
And how he'll manage, heaven knows,
  (My eyes are getting dim)
He says – he says – he don't – suppose
  I'll want to – to – marry – him.

As if I wouldn't take his hand
  Without a golden glove,
Oh! Jack, you men won't understand
  How much a girl can love.
I long to see his face once more –
  Jack's dog! Thank God, it's Jack –
(I never thought I'd faint before)
  He's coming up the track.

Henry Lawson, 1867-1922

It's Grand

It's grand to be a squatter
And sit upon a post,
And watch your little ewes and lambs
A-giving up the ghost.

It's grand to be a 'cockie'
With wife and kids to keep
And find an all-wise Providence
Has mustered all your sheep.

It's grand to be a Western man,
With shovel in your hand,
To dig your little homestead out
From underneath the sand.

It's grand to be a shearer,
Along the Darling side,
And pluck the wool from stinking sheep
That some days since have died.

It's grand to be a rabbit
And breed till all is blue,
And then to die in heaps because
There's nothing left to chew.

It's grand to be a Minister
And travel like a swell,
And tell the Central District folk
To go to – Inverell.

It's grand to be a Socialist
And lead the bold array
That marches to prosperity
At seven bob a day.

It's grand to be unemployed
And lie in the Domain,
And wake up every second day
And go to sleep again.

It's grand to borrow English tin
To pay for wharves and Rocks,
And then to find it isn't in
The little money-box.

It's grand to be a Democrat
And toady to the mob,
For fear that if you told the truth
They'd hunt you for your job.

It's grand to be a lot of things
In this fair Southern land,
But if the Lord would send us rain,
That would, indeed, be grand!

A.B. ('Banjo') Paterson, 1864-1941

The Shearing Shed

'The ladies are coming,' the super says
  To the shearers sweltering there,
And 'the ladies' means in the shearing-shed:
  'Don't cut 'em too bad. Don't swear.'
The ghost of a pause in the shed's rough heart,
  And lower is bowed each head;
Then nothing is heard save a whispered word
  And the roar of the shearing-shed.

The tall, shy rouser has lost his wits;
  His limbs are all astray;
He leaves a fleece on the shearing-board
  And his broom in the shearer's way.
There's a curse in store for that jackeroo
  As down by the wall he slants –
But the ringer bends with his legs askew
  And wishes he'd 'patched them pants'.

They are girls from the city. Our hearts rebel
  As we squint at their dainty feet,
While they gush and say in a girly way
  That 'the dear little lambs' are 'sweet'.
And Bill the Ringer, who'd scorn the use
  Of a childish word like damn,
Would give a pound that his tongue were loose
  As he tackles a lively lamb.

Swift thought of home in the coastal towns –
  Or rivers and waving grass –

And a weight on our hearts that we cannot define
  That comes as the ladies pass;
But the rouser ventures a nervous dig
  With his thumb in the next man's back;
And Bogan says to his pen-mate: 'Twig
  The style of that last un, Jack.'

Jack Moonlight gives her a careless glance –
  Then catches his breath with pain;
His strong hand shakes, and the sunbeams dance
  As he bends to his work again.
But he's well disguised in a bristling beard,
  Bronzed skin, and his shearer's dress;
And whatever he knew or hoped or feared
  Was hard for his mates to guess.

Jack Moonlight, wiping his broad, white brow,
  Explains with a doleful smile,
'A stitch in the side,' and 'I'm all right now' –
  But he leans on the beam awhile,
And gazes out in the blazing noon
  On the clearing brown and bare …
She had come and gone – like a breath of June
  In December's heat and glare.

Henry Lawson, 1867-1922

The Swagman

Oh, he was old and spare;
His bushy whiskers and his hair
Were all fussed up and very grey;
He said he'd come a long, long way
And had a long, long way to go.
Each boot was broken at the toe,
And he'd a swag upon his back,
His billy-can, as black as black,
Was just the thing for making tea
At picnics, so it seemed to me.

'Twas hard to earn a bit of bread,
He told me. Then he shook his head,
All the little corks that hung
Around his hat-brim danced and swung
And bobbed about his face; and when
I laughed he made them dance again.
He said they were for keeping flies –
'The pesky varmints' – from his eyes.
He called me 'Codger' . . . 'Now you see
The best days of your life,' said he.
'But days will come to bend your back
And, when they come, keep off the track,
Keep off, young codger, if you can.'

He seemed a funny sort of man.
He told me that he wanted work,
But jobs were scarce this side of Bourke,
And he supposed he'd have to go

Another fifty miles or so.
'Nigh all my life the track I've walked,'
He said. I liked the way he talked.
And oh, the places he had seen!
I don't know where he had not been –
On every road, in every town,
All through the country, up and down.
'Young codger, shun the track,' he said.
I noticed then that his old eyes
Were very blue and very wise.
'Ay, once I was a little lad,'
He said, and seemed to grow quite sad.

I sometimes think: When I'm a man,
I'll get a good black billy-can
And hang some corks around my hat,
And lead a jolly life like that.

C. J. Dennis, 1876-1938

Days When We Went Swimming

The breezes waved the silver grass
  Waist-high along the siding,
And to the creek we ne'er could pass,
  Three boys, on bareback riding;
Beneath the she-oaks in the bend
  The waterhole was brimming –
Do you remember yet, old friend,
  The times we went in swimming?

The days we played the wag from school –
  Joys shared – but paid for singly –
The air was hot, the water cool –
  And naked boys are kingly!
With mud for soap, the sun to dry –
  A well-planned lie to stay us,
And dust well rubbed on face and neck
  Lest cleanliness betray us.

And you'll remember farmer Kutz –
  Though scarcely for his bounty –
He'd leased a forty-acre block,
  And thought he owned the county;
A farmer of the old-world school,
  That men grew hard and grim in,
He drew his water from the pool
  That we preferred to swim in.

And do you mind when down the creek
  His angry way he wended,

A greenhide cartwhip in his hand
  For our young backs intended?
Three naked boys upon the sand –
  Half-buried and half-sunning
Three startled boys without their clothes
  Across the paddock running.

We'd had some scares, but we looked blank
  When, resting there and chumming
We glanced by chance across the bank
  And saw the farmer coming!
Some home impressions linger yet
  Of cups of sorrow brimming:
I hardly think that we'll forget
  The last day we went swimming.

Henry Lawson, 1867-1922

Been There Before

There came a stranger to Walgett town,
To Walgett town, when the sun was low,
And he carried a thirst that was worth a crown,
Yet how to quench it, he did not know;
But he thought he might take those yokels down,
The guileless yokels of Walgett town.

They made him a bet in a private bar,
In a private bar when the talk was high,

And they bet him some pounds no matter how far
He could pelt a stone, yet he could not shy
A stone right over the river so brown,
The Darling River at Walgett town.

He knew that the river from bank to bank
Was fifty yards, and he smiled a smile
As he tumbled down, but his hopes they sank
For there wasn't a stone within fifty mile;
For the saltbush plain and the open down
Produce no quarries in Walgett town.

The yokels laughed at his hopes o'erthrown,
And he stood awhile like a man in a dream;
Then out of his pocket he fetched a stone,
And pelted it over the silent stream –
He had been there before. He had wandered down
On a previous visit to Walgett town.

A.B. ('Banjo') Paterson, 1864-1941

The Sundowner

I know not where this tiresome man
With his shrewd, sable billy-can
And his unwashed Democracy
His boomed-up pilgrimage began.

Sometimes he wandered far outback
On a precarious Tucker Track;

Sometimes he lacked Necessities
No gentleman would like to lack.

Tall was the grass, I understand,
When the Squatter ruled the land.
Why were the Conquerors kind to him?
Ah, the Wax Matches in his hand!

Where bullockies with oaths intense
Made of the dragged-up trees a fence,
Gambling with scorpions he rolled
His Swag, conspicuous, immense.

In the full splendour of his power
Rarely he touched a mile an hour,
Dawdling at sunset, History says,
For the Pint Pannikin of flour.

Seldom he worked; he was, I fear,
Unreasonably slow and dear:
Little he earned, and that he spent
Deliberately drinking Beer.

Cheerfully, sorefooted child of chance,
Swiftly we knew him at a glance;
Boastful and self-compassionate,
Australia's Interstate Romance.

Shall he not live in Robust Rhyme,
Soliloquies and Odes Sublime?
Strictly between ourselves, he was
A rare old Humbug all the time.

In many a Book of Bushland dim
Mopokes shall give greeting grim:
The old swans pottering in the reeds
Shall pass the time of day to him.

In many a page our friend shall take
Small sticks his evening fire to make;
Shedding his waistcoat, he shall mix
On its smooth back his Johnny-Cake.

'Mid the dry leaves and silvery bark
Often at nightfall will he park
Close to a homeless creek, and hear
The Bunyip paddling in the dark.

John Shaw Neilson, 1872-1942

Five Miles from Gundagai

I'm used to punchin' bullock teams
Across the hills and plains,
I've teamed outback these forty years
In blazin' droughts and rains,
I've lived a heap of troubles down
Without a bloomin' lie,
But I can't forget what happened to me
Five miles from Gundagai.

'Twas getting dark, the team got bogged,
The axle snapped in two;
I lost me matches and me pipe,
So what was I to do?
The rain came on, 'twas bitter cold,
And hungry too was I.
And the dog sat on the tucker box
Five miles from Gundagai.

Some blokes I know has stacks o' luck,
No matter 'ow they fall,
But there was I, Lord love a duck!
No blasted luck at all.
I couldn't make a pot of tea,
Nor get me trousers dry,
And the dog sat on the tucker box
Five miles from Gundagai.

I can forgive the blinkin' team,

I can forgive the rain,
I can forgive the dark and cold,
And go through it again,
I can forgive me rotten luck,
But hang me till I die,
I can't forgive that bloody dog
Five miles from Gundagai.

Traditional

In Possum Land

In Possum Land the nights are fair,
The streams are fresh and clear;
No dust is in the moonlit air;
No traffic jars the ear.

With possums gambolling overhead,
'Neath western stars so grand,
Ah! Would that we could make our bed
Tonight in Possum Land.

Henry Lawson, 1867-1922

The Shakedown on the Floor

Set me back for twenty summers,
  For I'm tired of cities now –
Set my feet in red-soil furrows
  And my hands upon the plough,
With the two Black Brothers trudging
  On the home stretch through the loam
While along the grassy siding
  Come the cattle grazing home.

And I finish ploughing early,
  And I hurry home to tea –
There's my black suit on the stretcher,
  And a clean white shirt for me;
There's a dance at Rocky Rises,
  And, when they can dance no more,
For a certain favoured party
  There's a shakedown on the floor.

You remember Mary Carey,
  Bushman's favourite at The Rise?
With her sweet small freckled features,
  Red-gold hair, and kind grey eyes;
Sister, daughter, to her mother,
  Mother, sister to the rest –
And of all my friends and kindred
  Mary Carey loved me best.

Far too shy, because she loved me,
  To be dancing oft with me;

(What cared I, because she loved me,
　If the world were there to see?)
But we lingered by the sliprails
　While the rest were riding home,
Ere the hour before the dawning
　Dimmed the great star-clustered dome.

Small brown hands, that spread the mattress,
　While the old folk winked to see
How she'd find an extra pillow
　And an extra sheet for me.
For a moment shyly smiling,
　She would grant me one kiss more –
Slip away and leave me happy
　By the shakedown on the floor.

Rock me hard in steerage cabins,
　Rock me soft in first saloons,
Lay me on the sandhill lonely
　Under waning Western moons;
But wherever night may find me –
　Till I rest for evermore –
I shall dream that I am happy
　In the shakedown on the floor

Henry Lawson (1867-1922)

New Life, New Love

The cool breeze ripples the river below,
  And the fleecy clouds float high,
And I mark how the dark green gum-trees match
  The bright blue vault of the sky.
The rain has been, and the grass is green
  Where the slopes were bare and brown,
And I see the things that I used to see
  In the days ere my head went down.

I have found a light in my long dark night,
  Brighter than stars or moon;
I have lost the fear of the sunset drear,
  And the sadness of afternoon.
Here let us stand while I hold your hand,
  Where the light's on the your golden head –
Oh! I feel the thrill that I used to feel
  In the days ere my heart was dead.

The storm's gone by, but my lips are dry
  And the old wrong rankles yet –
Sweetheart or wife, I must take new life
  From your red lips warm and wet!
So let it be, you my cling to me,
  There is nothing on earth to dread,
For I'll be the man that I used to be
  In the days ere my heart were dead!

Henry Lawson, (1867-1922)

A Mountain Station

I bought a run a while ago
  On country rough and ridgy,
Where wallaroos and wombats grow –
  The Upper Murrumbidgee.
The grass is rather scant, it's true,
  But this a fair exchange is,
The sheep can see a lovely view
  By climbing up the ranges.

And She-oak Flat's the station's name,
  I'm not surprised at that, sirs:
The oaks were there before I came,
  And I supplied the flat, sirs.
A man would wonder how it's done,
  The stock so soon decreases –
They sometimes stumble off the run
  And break themselves to pieces.

I've tried to make expenses meet,
  But wasted all my labours;
The sheep the dingoes didn't eat
  Were stolen by the neighbours.
They stole my pears – my native pears –
  Those thrice-convicted felons,
And ravished from me unawares
  My crop of paddy-melons.

And sometimes under sunny skies,
  Without an explanation,
The Murrumbidgee used to rise
  And overflow the station.
But this was caused (as I now know)
  When summer sunshine glowing
Had melted all Kiandra's snow
  And set the river going.

Then in the news, perhaps, you read:
  'Stock Passings. Puckawidgee,
Fat cattle: Seven hundred head
  Swept down the Murrumbidgee:'
Their destination's quite obscure,
  But, somehow, there's a notion,
Unless the river falls, they're sure
  To reach the Southern Ocean.

So after that I'll give it best;
  No more with Fate I'll battle.
I'll let the river take the rest,
  For those were all my cattle.
And with one comprehensive curse
  I close my brief narration,
And advertise it in my verse –
  'For Sale! A Mountain Station.'

A..B ('Banjo') Paterson (1864-1941)

Emus

My annals have it so:
A thing my mother saw,
Nigh eighty years ago,
With happiness and awe.

Along a level hill —
A clearing in wild space,
And night's last tardy chill
Yet damp on morning's face.

Sight never to forget:
Solemn against the sky
In stately silhouette
Ten emus walking by.

One after one they went
In line, and without haste:
On their unknown intent,
Ten emus grandly paced.

She, used to hedged-in fields,
Watched them go filing past
Into the great Bush Wilds
Silent and vast.

Sudden that hour she knew
That this far place was good,
This mighty land and new
For soul's hardihood.

For hearts that love the strange,
That carry wonder;
The Bush, the hills, the range,
And the dark flats under.

Mary Fullerton, 1868-1946

A Singer of the Bush

There is waving of grass in the breeze
And a song in the air,
And a murmur of myriad bees
That toil everywhere.
There is scent in the blossom and bough,
And the breath of the Spring
Is as soft as a kiss on the brow
And Springtime I sing.

There is drought on the land, and the stock
Tumble down in their tracks
Or follow – a tottering flock –
The scrub-cutter's axe.
While ever a creature survives
The axes shall swing;
We are fighting with fate for their lives –
And the combat I sing.

A. B. ('Banjo') Paterson, 1864-1941

The Teams

A cloud of dust on the long, white road,
  And teams go creeping on
Inch by inch with the weary load;
  And by the power of the greenhide goad
The distant goal is won.

With eyes half-shut to the blinding dust,
  And necks to the yokes bent low,
The beasts are pulling as bullocks must;
  And the shining tyres might almost rust
While the spokes are turning slow.

With face half-hid by a broad-brimmed hat,
  That shades from the heat's white waves,
And shouldered whip, with its greenhide plait,
  The driver plods with a gait like that
Of his weary, patient slaves.

He wipes his brow, for the day is hot,
  And spits to the left with spite;
He shouts at Bally, and flicks at Scott,
  And raises dust from the back of Spot,
And spits to the dusty right.

He'll sometimes pause as a thing of form
  In front of a settler's door,
And ask for a drink, and remark, 'It's warm,'
  Or say 'There's sign of a thunderstorm;'
But he seldom utters more.

The rains are heavy on roads like these
  And, fronting his lonely home,
For days together the settler sees
  The wagons bogged to the axletrees,
Or ploughing the sodden loam.

And then, when the roads are at their worst,
  The bushman's children hear
The cruel blows of the whips reversed
  While the bullocks pull as their hearts would burst,
And bellow with pain and fear.

And thus – with glimpses of home and rest –
  Are the long, long journeys done;
And thus – 'tis a thankless life at best! –
  Is Distance fought in the mighty West,
And the lonely battle won.

Henry Lawson, 1867-1922

Down the River

I've done with joys an' misery,
An' why should I repine?
There's no one knows the past but me
An' that ol' dog o' mine.
We camp, an' walk, an' camp an' walk,
An find it fairly good;
He can do anything but talk –
An' wouldn't, if he could.

We sits an' thinks beside the fire,
With all the stars a-shine,
An' no one knows our thoughts but me
An that there dog o' mine.
We has our Johnny-cake an' scrag,
An' finds 'em fairly good;
He can do anything but talk –
An' wouldn't if he could.

I has my smoke, he has his rest,
When sunset's getting dim;
An' if I do get drunk at times,
It's all the same to him.
So long's he's got my swag to mind,
He thinks that times is good;
He can do anything but talk –
An' wouldn't if he could.

Henry Lawson, 1867-1922

Rain in the Mountains

The valley's full of misty clouds,
Its tinted beauty drowning,
Tree-tops are veiled in fleecy shrouds,
And mountain fronts are frowning.

The mist is hanging like a pall
Above the granite ledges,
And many a silvery waterfall
Leaps o'er the valley's edges.

The sky is of a leaden grey,
Save where the north looks surly,
The driven daylight speeds away,
And night come o'er us early.

Dear Love, the rain will pass full soon,
Far sooner than my sorrow,
But in a golden afternoon
The sun may set tomorrow.

Henry Lawson, 1867-1922

The Stirrup Song

We've drunk our wine, we've kissed our girls, and
 funds are getting low,
The horses must be thinking it's a fair thing now to go.
Sling up the swags on Condamine, and strap the
 billies fast,
And stuff a bottle in the bag, and let's be off at last.

What matter if the creeks are up! – the cash, alas,
 runs down! –
A very sure and certain sign we're long enough in town;
The black man rides the 'boko' and you'd better take
 the bay,
Quartpot will do to carry me the stage we'll go today.

No grass this side the Border fence, and all the
 mulga's dead;
The horses for a day or two will have to spiel ahead;
Man never yet from Queensland brought a bullock
 or a hack
But lost condition on that God-abandoned Border track:

But once we're through the rabbit-proof, it's certain
 since the rain
There's whips of grass and water, so it's 'West-by-
North' again;
There's feed on Tyson country, we can spell the
 mokes a week
Where Bill Stevens last year trapped his brumbies on
 Bough Creek.

The Paroo may be quickly crossed – the Eulo
  Common's bare –
And anyhow it isn't wise, old man, to dally there!
Alack-a-day! far wiser men than you or I succumb
To a woman's wiles and potency of Queensland
  wayside rum!

Then over sand and spinifex and o'er range and
  plain!
The nags are fresh; besides they know they're
  westward bound again!
The brand upon old Darkie's thigh is that upon the
  hide
Of bullocks we shall muster on the Diamantina side.

We'll light our campfires while we may, and yarn
  beside the blaze,
The jingling hobble-chains shall make a music
  through the days;
And while the tucker-bags are right and we've a
  stock of weed
The swagman will be welcome to a pipeful and a feed.

So fill your pipe, and ere we mount we'll drain
  a parting nip;
Here's how that West-by-North again may prove a
  lucky trip;
Then back once more, let's trust you'll find your best
  girl's merry face,
Or, if she jilts you, may you get a better in her place.

Harry ('The Breaker') Morant, 1865-1902

Freedom on the Wallaby

Our fathers toiled for bitter bread
While idlers thrived beside them;
But food to eat and clothes to wear
Their native land deprived them.
They left their native land in spite
Of royalty's regalia,
And so they came, or if they stole,
Were sent out to Australia.

They struggled hard to make a home,
Hard grubbing 'twas and clearing.
They weren't troubled much with toffs
When they were pioneering:
And now that we have made the land
A garden full of promise,
Old greed must crook his dirty hand
And come and take if from us.

But Freedom's on the Wallaby,
She'll knock the tyrants silly,
She's going to light another fire
And boil another billy.
We'll make the tyrants feel the sting
Of those that they would throttle;
They needn't say the fault is ours
If blood should stain the wattle.

Henry Lawson, 1867-1922

The Last Sundowner

He sat upon a fallen log,
And heaved a long, deep sigh.
His gnarled hand fondling his old dog
As his gaze went to the sky.
'There goes another plane,' said he –
'A soarin', roarin' pest!'
They robs a man of privacy,
An' motor cars of rest.

'Sundownin' ain't the game it was
Since men have took to wings;
An' life grows narrer, jist because
Of planes an' cars an' things.
For the planes have pinched me private skies
An' the cars have grabbed me earth
An' all the news by wireless flies;
So what's sundownin' worth?

'Time was when I could sit me down
Where man had left no sign,
An' earth an' sky for miles aroun'
For that one hour was mine.
And I could sit an' think me thorts
An' watch the sun go west
Without no crazy ingine's snorts
To break into me rest.

'And as the afternoon grew late
I'd seek the haunts of men.

An' at some lonely homestead gate
I'd have sure welcome then;
An' tucker-bags were gladly filled
And rest found for my back,
In change for bits of news I spilled
And gossip of the track.

'But now that wireless spreads its lies
From this and other lands,
They look on me with hard, cold eyes
An' give with grudgin' hands.
It's them that has to give me news;
And when I seek some wide,
Once silent scene, planes spoil me views,
An' cars honk me aside.'

He sat upon a fallen log
And heaved a long, deep sigh,
'We're agein', me and me ole dog,
An' old things have to die.
Sundownin's dead: men's minds an' ways
Is changin' with a jerk.
Seems like I'll have to end me days
Travellin', in search of work.'

C. J. Dennis, 1876-1938

Camping

O Scents from dewy grass and tree;
O fluting birds at morn,
Loud, jubilant, or broken-sweet;
O Cloudlets fleecy, torn,
Floating on the fields of azure blue
Far in the distance, low!
I think of these and raptured cry:
A-camping we will go!

With every waft from greening earth
Wet with a gentle shower;
With every moving in the trees;
With every dancing flower;
I hear a song within my breast,
Over wide spaces, and I sigh:
A-camping we will go!

By murmuring streams and fountain falls;
By ferny hills and dales;
By shadowed cleft and hidden cave,
And old forgotten trails;
By bending, perfumed lilied brake;
By waves in endless flow;
I'll sing as on the grass I lie:
A-camping we will go!

By flaming multitudes of stars,
Unvalued of most men,
Offering ephemerals purged might,

Aeries of prison-den;
By crescent moons soaring above
All beauty that I know—
A lover to the bush I'll fly:
A-camping we will go!

Barcroft Boake, 1866-1892

Progress

They've builded wooden timber tracks,
And a trolley with screaming breaks
Noses into the secret bush,
Into the birdless brooding bush,
And the tall old gums it takes.

And down the sunny valley
The snorting saw screams slow;
Oh, bush that nursed my people,
Oh, bush that cursed my people,
I weep to watch you go.

'Furnley Maurice' (Frank Wilmot) 1881-1942

Bush Songs & Ballads

The Wild Colonial Boy

'Tis of a wild colonial boy,
Jack Doolan was his name,
Of poor but honest parents
Who lived in Castlemaine,
He was his father's only hope,
His mother's pride and joy,
And dearly did his parents love
Their wild colonial boy.

Chorus:
So come all my hearties,
We'll roam the mountains high,
Together we will plunder,
Together we will ride.
We'll scour along the valleys
And gallop o'er the plains,
And scorn to live in slavery,
Bound down with chains.

He was scarcely sixteen years of age
When he left his native home,
And through Australia's sunny clime
A bushranger did roam.
He robbed those wealthy squatters,
Their stock he did destroy,
And a terror to Australia
Was the wild colonial boy.

In 'sixty-one this daring youth
Commenced his wild career,
With courage all undaunted,
No foreman did he fear.
He stuck up the Beechworth mail-coach
And robbed Judge McEvoy,
Who, trembling cold, gave up his gold,
To the wild colonial boy.

He bade the judge, 'Good morning,'
And told him to beware,
That he'd never rob a hearty chap
Who acted on the square.
And never rob a mother of
Her son and only joy,
Or else he might turn outlaw like
That wild colonial boy.

One day as he was riding
The mountainside along,
A-listening to the little birds,
Their pleasant laughing song,
Three mounted troopers rode along,
Kelly, Davis and Fitzroy,
With a warrant for the capture
Of the wild colonial boy.

'Surrender now, Jack Doolan,
You see we're three to one,
Surrender in the Queen's name,
You daring highwayman!'

He pulled a pistol from his belt
And waved the little toy,
'I'll fight but not surrender!'
Cried the wild colonial boy.

He fired at trooper Kelly,
And brought him to the ground,
But in return, from Davis,
Received his mortal wound,
All shattered through the jaw he lay,
Still firing at Fitzroy,
And that's the way they captured him,
The wild colonial boy.

Traditional

Brave Ben Hall

Come all Australian sons with me,
For a hero has been slain
And cowardly butchered in his sleep
Upon the Lachlan plain.

Pray do not stay your seemly grief,
But let a teardrop fall
For many hearts shall always mourn
The fate of bold Ben Hall.

No brand of Cain e'er stamped his brow,
No widow's curse did fall;
When tales are read, the squatters dread
The name of bold Ben Hall.

The records of this hero bold
Through Europe have been heard,
And formed a conversation
Between many an Earl and Lord.

Ever since the good old days
Of Dick Turpin and Duval,
Knights of the road were outlaws bold,
And so was bold Ben Hall.

He never robbed a needy man,
His records best will show,
Staunch and loyal to his mates,
And manly to the foe.

Until he left his trusty mates,
The cause I ne'er could hear,
The bloodhounds of the law heard this
And after him did steer.

They found his place of ambush,
And cautiously they crept,
And savagely they murdered him
While the victim slept.

Yes, savagely they murdered him,
The cowardly blue-coat imps,
Who were led onto where he slept
By informing peelers' pimps.

No more he'll mount his gallant steed,
Nor range the mountains high,
The widow's friend in poverty –
Bold Ben Hall, good-bye.

Traditional

The Streets of Forbes

Come all you Lachlan men,
A sorrowful tale I'll tell
Concerning a bold hero
Who through misfortune fell.
His name it was Ben Hall,

A man of great renown,
Who was hunted from his station
And like a dog shot down.

Three years he roamed the highway
And had a lot of fun,
A thousand pounds was on his head,
With Gilbert and John Dunn.
Ben parted from his comrades;
The outlaws did agree
To give up their bushranging
And cross the briny sea.

Ben went to Goobang Creek,
And this was his downfall;
For riddled like a sieve
Was valiant Ben Hall.
It was early in the morning
Upon the fifth of May,
When the police surrounded him
As fast asleep he lay.

Bill Dargin he was chosen
To shoot the outlaw dead;
The troopers fired madly
And filled him full of lead.
They threw him on his horse
And strapped him like a swag,
Then led him through the streets of Forbes
To show the prize they had!

Jack McGuire

The Death of Ben Hall

Ben Hall was out on the Lachlan side
With a thousand pounds on his head;
A score of troopers were scattered wide
And a hundred more were ready to ride
Wherever a rumour led.

They had followed his track from the Weddin heights
And north by the Weelong yards
Through dazzling days and moonlit nights
They had sought him over their rifle-sights,
With their hands on their trigger-guards.

The outlaw stole like a hunted fox
Through the scrub and stunted heath,
And peered like a hawk from his eyrie rocks
Through the waving boughs of the sapling box
On the troopers riding beneath.

His clothes were rent by the clutching thorn
And his blistered feet were bare;
Ragged and torn, with his beard unshorn,
He hid in the woods like a beast forlorn,
With a padded path to his lair.

But every night when the white stars rose
He crossed by the Gunning Plain
To a stockman's hut where the Gunning flows,
And struck on the door three swift light blows,
And a hand unhooked the chain –

And the outlaw followed the lone path back
With food for another day;
And the kindly darkness covered his track
And the shadows swallowed him deep and black
Where the starlight melted away.

But his friend had read of the Big Reward,
And his soul was stirred with greed;
He fastened his door and window-board,
He saddled his horse and crossed the ford,
And spurred to the town at speed.

You may ride at a man's or a maid's behest
When honour or true love call
And steel your heart to the worst or best,
But the ride that is ta'en on a traitor's quest
Is the bitterest ride of all.

A hot wind blew from the Lachlan bank
And a curse on its shoulder came;
The pine-trees frowned at him, rank on rank,
The sun on a gathering storm-cloud sank
And flushed his cheek with shame.

He reined at the Court; and the tale began
That the rifles alone should end;
Sergeant and trooper laid their plan
To draw the net on a hunted man
At the treacherous word of a friend.

False was the hand that raised the chain
And false was the whispered word;

'The troopers have turned to the south again,
You may dare to camp on the Gunning Plain.'
And the weary outlaw heard.

He walked from the hut but a quarter-mile
Where a clump of saplings stood
In a sea of grass like a lonely isle;
And the moon came up in a little while
Like silver steeped in blood.

Ben Hall lay down on the dew-wet ground
By the side of his tiny fire;
And a night breeze woke, and he heard no sound
As the troopers drew their cordon round –
And the traitor earned his hire.

And nothing they saw in the dim grey light,
But the little glow in the trees;
And they crouched in the tall cold grass all night,
Each one ready to shoot at sight,
With his rifle cocked on his knees.

When the shadows broke and the dawn's white sword
Swung over the mountain wall,
And a little wind blew over the ford,
A sergeant sprang to his feet and roared:
'In the name of the Queen, Ben Hall!'

Haggard, the outlaw leapt from his bed
With his lean arms held on high.
'Fire!' And the word was scarcely said
When the mountains rang to a rain of lead –

And the dawn went drifting by.

They kept their word and they paid his pay
Where a clean man's hand would shrink;
And that was the traitor's master-day
As he stood by the bar on his homeward way
And called on the crowd to drink.

He banned no creed and he banned no class,
And he called to his friends by name;
But the worst would shake his head and pass
And none would drink from the bloodstained glass
And the goblet red with shame.

And I know when I hear the last grim call
And my mortal hour is spent,
When the light is hid and the curtains fall
I would rather sleep with the dead Ben Hall
Than go where that traitor went.

Anonymous

Ballad of Ben Hall's Gang

Come all you wild colonials
And listen to my tale;
A story of bushrangers' deeds
I will to you unveil.
'Tis of those gallant heroes,

Game fighters one and all;
And we'll sit and sing, 'Long live the King,
Dunn, Gilbert and Ben Hall.'

Frank Gardiner was a bushranger
Of terrible renown;
He robbed the Forbes gold escort,
And eloped with Kitty Brown,
But in the end they lagged him,
Two-and-thirty years in all.
'We must avenge the Darkie,'
Says Dunn, Gilbert and Ben Hall.

Ben Hall was a squatter
Who owned six hundred head;
A peaceful man was he until
Arrested by Sir Fred.
His home burned down, his wife cleared out;
His cattle perished all.
'They'll not take me a second time,'
Says valiant Ben Hall.

John Gilbert was a flash cove,
And John O'Meally too;
With Ben and Burke and Johnny Vane
They all were comrades true.
They rode into Canowindra
And gave a public ball.
'Roll up, roll up, and have a spree,'
Says Gilbert and Ben Hall.

They took possession of the town,

Including public houses
And treated all the cockatoos
And shouted for their spouses
They danced with all the pretty girls
And held a carnival.
'We don't hurt them who don't hurt us,'
Says Gilbert and Ben Hall.

Then Miss O'Flanagan performed
In manner quite genteelly
Upon the grand pianner
For the bushranger O'Meally.
'Roll up! Roll up! Its' just a lark
For women, kids and all;
We'll rob the rich and help the poor,'
Says Gilbert and Ben Hall.

They made a raid on Bathurst,
The pace was getting hot;
But Johnny Vane surrendered
After Micky Burke was shot.
O'Meally at Goimbla
Did like a hero fall;
'The game is getting lively,'
Says Gilbert and Ben Hall.

Then Gilbert took a holiday,
Ben Hall got new recruits;
The Old Man and Dunleavy
Shared in the plunder's fruits.
Dunleavy he surrendered

And they jugged the Old Man tall –
So Johnny Gilbert came again
To help his mate, Ben Hall.

John Dunn he was a jockey,
A-riding all the winners,
Until he joined Hall's gang to rob
The publicans and sinners;
And many a time the Royal Mail
Bailed up at John Dunn's call,
A thousand pounds is on their heads –
Dunn, Gilbert and Ben Hall.

'Hand over all your watches
And the banknotes in your purses.
All travellers must pay toll to us;
We don't care for your curses.
We are the rulers of the roads,
We've seen the troopers fall,
And we want your gold and money,'
Says Dunn, Gilbert and Ben Hall.

'Next week we'll visit Goulburn
And clean the banks out there;
So if you see the peelers,
 Just tell them to beware;
Some day to Sydney city
We mean to pay a call,
And we'll take the whole damn country,'
Says Dunn, Gilbert and Ben Hall.

Anonymous

The Bloody Field of Wheogo

The moon rides high in a starry sky,
And, through the midnight gloom,
A faery scene of woodland green
Her silver rays illume.

Dark mountains show a ridge of snow
Against the deep blue sky,
And a winding stream with sparkling gleam
Flows merrily murmuring by.

Not a sound is heard, save a bough when stirred
By the night-wind's moaning sigh,
Or, piercing and shrill, echoed back by the hill,
A curlew's mournful cry.

A twinkling bright in the shadowy night
A lonely taper shines,
And seated there is a wanton fair
Who in amorous sadness pines.

For her lord is gone, and she sits alone,
Alone in her mountain home.
For 'twas not her lord that she deplored,
For she liked to see him roam.

The joy of her heart is a bushranger smart
Who, lion-like, prowls in the night:
And with supper all spread, and a four-post bed,
She waits by the flickering light.

Equipped for fight, in trappings bright,
Came a band of warriors there,
By gallant Sir Fred right gallantly led,
The 'ranger to seize in a snare.

They spread all around, and the house they surround,
Nine men with revolver and gun;
'A reward's on his head!' cried the gallant Sir Fred,
'And we're nine to the bushranger's one!'

Still gleamed the light in the shades of night,
And still the pale moon shone;
But no 'ranger came to cheer the dame
As she sat by the window alone.

The warriors bold were freezing with cold,
And wished they were in their beds,
When the echoing beat of a horse's feet
Sent the blood in a rush to their heads!

At gentle speed on snow-white steed
And singing a joyous song
To the beckoning light in the shadowy night
The bushranger rides along.

A stalwart man was he to scan,
And flushed with ruffian pride;
In many a fray he had won the day
And the 'New Police' had defied.

Up started then Sir Fred and his men
With cocked carbines in hand

And called aloud to the 'ranger proud
On pain of death to 'stand'.

But the 'ranger proud, he laughed aloud,
And bounding rode away,
While Sir Frederick Pott shut his eye for a shot
And missed – in his usual way.

His troopers then like valiant men
With their carbines blazed away.
The whistling lead on its mission sped,
But whither, none can say.

The snow-white steed at gentle speed
Bore the 'ranger from their view
And left Sir Fred to return to bed –
There was nothing else to do.

But Sir Frederick Pott with rage was hot
As he looked at his warriors eight.
They were nine to one, with revolver and gun!
He cursed his luckless fate.

He shuddered to think how his glory would sink
When the country heard of the mess
And the tale was told of his exploit bold
In the columns of the Press.

In fury then he marched his men
To the home of the wanton fair.
With warlike din they entered in
To search and ransack there.

In slumber sound a boy they found,
And brave Sir Frederick said:
'By a flash in the pan we missed the man,
So we'll take the boy instead!'

Anonymous

The Maids of the Mountains

In the wild Weddin Mountains
There live two young dames,
Kate O'Meally, Bet Mayhew
Are their pretty names.
These maids of the mountains
Are bonny bush belles:
They ride out on horseback
Togged out like young swells.

They dressed themselves up
In their brothers' best clothes
And looked very rakish
As you may suppose
In the joy of their hearts
They chuckled with glee –
What fun if for robbers
They taken should be.

Just then the policemen,
By day and by night,

Were seeking Frank Gardiner,
The bushranger sprite.
Bold Constable Clark
Wore a terrible frown
As he thought how Sir Freddy
By Frank was done down.

They sought for the 'ranger
But of course found him not,
When suddenly Katy
And Betsy they spot.
'By Pott,' shouted Clark,
'That is Gardiner I see!
The wretch must be taken;
Come, boys, follow me!'

'Stand!' shouted the bobbies
In accents most dread,
'Or else you will taste
Our infallibe lead!'
But the maids of the mountains
Just laughed at poor Clark,
And galloped away
To continue their lark.

The troopers pursued them,
And hot was the chase;
'Tis only at Randwick
They go such a pace.
Clark captured the pair,
Then, to show his vexation,

He lugged them both off
To the Young police station.

The maids of the mountains
The joke much enjoyed,
To see their brave captors
So sadly annoyed.
Next day they still smiled
As they stood in the dock;
Their awful position
Their nerves did not shock.

But Constable Clark
Did not look very jolly;
He had no excuse
For such absolute folly.
He admitted the girls
Were just out on a spree
And hoped that His Worship
Would set them both free.

And so the farce ended
Of Belles versus Blues,
Which caused no great harm
And did much to amuse,
But the Burrangong bobbies
Will place in the cells
No more maids of the mountains –
The bonny bush belles.

Anonymous

Frank Gardiner He is Caught at Last

Frank Gardiner he is caught at last
And now in Sydney jail –
For wounding Sergeant Middleton
And robbing the Mudgee mail,
For plundering of the escort
And Cargo mail also,
It was for gold he made so bold
And not so long ago.

His daring deeds surprised them all
Throughout the Sydney land;
He gave a call unto his friends
And quickly raised a band.
Fortune always favoured him
Until the time of late;
There was Burke, the brave O'Meally too,
Met with a dreadful fate.

Young Johnny Vane surrendered,
Ben Hall received some wounds;
And as for Johnny Gilbert,
At Binalong he was found.
Alone he was, he lost his horse,
Three troopers hove in sight;
He fought the three most manfully,
Got slaughtered in the fight.

Farewell adieu to outlawed Frank
He was the poor man's friend;
The Government has secured him,
The laws he did offend.
He boldly stood his trial
And answered in a breath
'And do what you will, you can but kill,
I have no fear of death!'

Fresh charges brought against him
From neighbours near and far
Day after day they remanded him,
Escorted from the bar.
And now it is all over
The sentence it is passed
Reprieving from the gallows cursed
This highwayman at last.

When lives you take – a warning boys –
A woman never trust;
She will turn round, I will be bound,
Queen's evidence the first.
Two and thirty years he's doomed
To slave all for the Crown;
And well may he say he cursed the day
He met old Mother Brown.

Anonymous

The Diverting History of John Gilbert

John Gilbert was a bushranger
Of terrible renown
For sticking lots of people up,
And shooting others down.

John Gilbert said unto his pals,
'Although they make a bobbery
About our tricks, we've never done
A tip-top thing in robbery.

'We've all of us a fancy for
Experiments in pillage;
But never have we seized a town,
 Or even sacked a village.'

John Gilbert stated to his mates,
'Though partners we have been
In all rascality, yet we
No festal day have seen.'

John Gilbert said he thought he saw
No obstacle to hinder a
Piratical descent upon
The town of Canowindra.

So into Canowindra town
Rode Gilbert and his men

And all the Canowindra folk
Subsided there and then.

The Canowindra populace
Cried, 'Here's a lot of strangers,'
But suddenly recovered when
They found they were bushrangers.

John Gilbert and his partisans
Said, 'Don't you be afraid –
We are but old companions whom
Rank outlaws you have made.'

So Johnny Gilbert says, says he,
'We'll never hurt a hair
Of men who bravely recognise
That we are just and fair.'

The New South Welshmen said at once,
Not making any fuss,
That Johnny Gilbert after all
Was 'just but one of us.'

So Johnny Gilbert took the town
And took the public houses,
And treated all the cockatoos
And shouted for their spouses.

And Miss O'Flanagan performed
In manner quite 'ginteelly'
Upon the grand piano for
The bushranger O'Meally.

And every stranger passing by
They took, and when they'd got him,
They robbed him of his money, and
Occasionally they shot him.

And Johnny's enigmatic freak
Admits of this solution,
Bushranging is in New South Wales
A favoured institution.

So Johnny Gilbert ne'er allows
An anxious thought to fetch him,
Because he knows the Government
Don't really want to catch him.

And if such practices should be
To New South Welshmen dear,
With not the least demurring word
Ought we to interfere?

Anonymous

How Gilbert Died

There's never a stone at the sleeper's head,
There's never a fence beside,
And the wandering stock on the grave may tread
Unnoticed and undenied;
But the smallest child on the Watershed
Can tell you how Gilbert died.

For he rode at dusk with his comrade Dunn
To the hut at the Stockman's Ford;
In the waning light of the sinking sun
They peered with a fierce accord.
They were outlaws both – and on each man's head
Was a thousand pounds reward.

They had taken toll of the country round,
And the troopers came behind
With a black that tracked like a human hound
In the scrub and ranges blind;
He could run the trail where a white man's eye
No sign of a track could find.

He had hunted them out of One Tree Hill
And over the Old Man Plain,
But they wheeled their tracks with a wild beast's
  skill,
And they made for the range again;
Then away to the hut where their grandsire dwelt
They rode with a loosened rein.

And their grandsire gave them a greeting bold:
'Come in and rest in peace,
No safer place does the country hold –
With the night pursuit must cease,
And we'll drink success to the roving boys,
And to hell with the black police.'

But they went to death when they entered there
In the hut at the Stockman's Ford,
For their grandsire's words were as false as fair –
They were doomed to the hangman's cord.
He had sold them both to the black police
For the sake of the big reward.

In the depth of the night there are forms that glide
As stealthy as serpents creep,
And around the hut where the outlaws hide
They plant in the shadows deep,
And they wait till the first faint flush of dawn
Shall waken their prey from sleep.

But Gilbert wakes while the night is dark –
A restless sleeper aye,
He has heard the sound of a sheep-dog's bark,
And his horse's warning neigh,
And he says to his mate 'There are hawks abroad,
And it's time we went away.'

Their rifles stood at the stretcher head,
Their bridles lay to hand;
They wakened the old man out of his bed,
When they heard the sharp command:

'In the name of the Queen, lay down your arms,
Now, Dunn and Gilbert, stand!'

Then Gilbert reached for his rifle true
That close at hand he kept;
He pointed straight at the voice, and drew,
But never a flash outleapt,
For the water ran from the rifle breech –
It was drenched while the outlaws slept.

Then he dropped the piece with a bitter oath,
And he turned to his comrade Dunn;
'We are sold,' he said, 'we are dead men both,
But there may be a chance for one;
I'll stop and fight with the pistol here,
You take to your heels and run.'

So Dunn crept out on his hands and knees
In the dim, half-dawning light,
And he made his way to a patch of trees,
And was lost in the black of night;
And the trackers hunted his tracks all day,
But they never could trace his flight.

But Gilbert walked from the open door
In a confident style and rash;
He heard at his side the rifles roar,
And he heard the bullets crash,
But he laughed as he lifted his pistol-hand,
And he fired at the rifle flash.

Then out of the shadows the troopers aimed

At his voice and the pistol sound.
With rifle flashes the darkness flamed –
He staggered and spun around,
And they riddled his body with rifle balls
As it lay on the blood-soaked ground.

There's never a stone at the sleeper's head,
There's never a fence beside,
And the wandering stock on the grave may tread
Unnoticed and undenied;
But the smallest child on the Watershed
Can tell you how Gilbert died.

A.B. ('Banjo') Paterson, 1864-1941

The Death of Morgan

Throughout Australian history
No tongue or pen can tell
Of such preconcerted treachery –
There is no parallel –
As the tragic deed of Morgan's death;
Without warning he was shot
On Peechelba station,
It will never be forgot.

I have oft-times heard of murders
In Australia's golden land,

But such an open daylight scene
Of thirty in a band.
Assembled at the dawn of day,
And then to separate,
Behind the trees, some on their knees,
Awaiting Morgan's fate.

Too busy was the servant-maid;
She trotted half the night
From Macpherson's down to Rutherford's
The tidings to recite.
A messenger was sent away
Who for his neck had no regard,
He returned with a troop of traps
In hopes of their reward.

But they were all disappointed;
Mr McQuinlan was the man
Who fired from his rifle
And shot rebellious Dan.
Concealed he stood behind a tree
Till his victim came in view,
And as Morgan passed his doom was cast –
The unhappy man he slew.

There was a rush for trophies,
Soon as the man was dead;
They cut off his beard, his ears,
And half the hair from his head,
In truth it was a hideous sight
As he struggled on the ground,

They tore the clothes from off his back
And exposed the fatal wound.

Oh, Morgan was the traveller's friend;
The squatters all rejoice
That the outlaw's life is at en end,
No more they'll hear his voice.
Success attend all highwaymen
Who do the poor some good;
But my curse attend a treacherous man
Who'd shed another's blood.

Farewell to Burke, O'Meally,
Young Gilbert and Ben Hall,
Likewise to Daniel Morgan,
Who fell by rifle-ball;
So all young men be warned
And never take up arms,
Remember this, how true it is,
Bushranging hath no charms!

Anonymous

Over the Border

Over the border to rifle and plunder,
Over the border went Morgan the bold,
Over the border, a terrible blunder,
For over the border bold Morgan lies cold.

Over the border, why, why did he wander
'Midst cold-hearted strangers all friendless to roam?
Was it that absence might make him grow fonder
Of those he had left in his own native home?

Over the border not long, did he plunder,
Swift is stern justice as slow she is here,
Bold are the men o'er the border, no wonder,
When even the women know nothing of fear.

Fiercely they hunt him the cruel marauder.
Quickly they follow him, dead on his track,
Line with their troopers the river-side border,
Over he may come, but never go back.

Never – from far and near gathering quickly,
Stern faces watch him all night through the gloom,
Nought can avail him now sympathy sickly,
Sealed is forever the murderer's doom.

Shot like a dog in the bright early morning,
Shot without mercy who mercy had none,
Like a wild beast without challenge or warning.
Soon his career of dark villainy's run.

Honour the brave hearts there over the border,
Great was the lesson they taught us that day;
Oh! that each other bushranging marauder,
Over the border would venture to stray.

Anonymous

The Man from Snowy River

There was movement at the station, for the word had
  passed around
That the colt from old Regret had got away,
And had joined the wild bush horses – he was worth
  a thousand pound,
So all the cracks had gathered to the fray.
All the tried and noted riders from the stations near
  and far
Had mustered at the homestead overnight,
For the bushmen love hard riding where the wild
  bush horses are,
And the stock-horse snuffs the battle with delight.

There was Harrison, who made his pile when Pardon
  won the cup,
The old man with his hair as white as snow;
But few could ride beside him when his blood was
  fairly up –
He would go wherever horse and man could go.
And Clancy of the Overflow came down to lend
  a hand,
No better horseman ever held the reins;
For never horse could throw him while the saddle-
  girths would stand –
He learnt to ride while droving on the plains.

And one was there, a stripling on a small and weedy
  beast;
He was something like a racehorse undersized,

With a touch of Timor pony – three parts thorough
  bred at least –
And such as are by mountain horsemen prized.
He was hard and tough and wiry – just the sort that
  won't say die—
There was courage in his quick impatient tread;
And he bore the badge of gameness in his bright
  and fiery eye,
And the proud and lofty carriage of his head.

But still so slight and weedy, one would doubt his
  power to stay,
And the old man said, 'That horse will never do
For a long and tiring gallop – lad, you'd better stop
  away,
Those hills are far too rough for such as you.'
So he waited, sad and wistful – only Clancy stood
  his friend –
'I think we ought to let him come,' he said;
'I warrant he'll be with us when he's wanted at the
  end,
For both his horse and he are mountain bred.

'He hails from Snowy River, up by Kosciusko side,
Where the hills are twice as steep and twice as
  rough;
Where a horse's hoofs strike firelight from the flint
  stones every stride,
The man that holds his own is good enough.
And the Snowy River riders on the mountains make
  their home,

Where the river runs those giant hills between;
I have seen full many horsemen since I first
  commenced to roam,
But nowhere yet such horsemen have I seen.'

So he went; they found the horses by the big
  mimosa clump,
They raced away towards the mountain's brow,
And the old man gave his orders, 'Boys, go at them
  from the jump,
No use to try for fancy riding now.
And, Clancy, you must wheel them, try and wheel
  them to the right.
For never yet was rider that could keep the mob
  in sight,
If once they gain the shelter of those hills.'

So Clancy rode to wheel them – he was racing
  on the wing
Where the best and boldest riders take their place,
And he raced his stock-horse past them, and he
  made the ranges ring
With the stockwhip, as he met them face to face.
Then they halted for a moment, while he swung the
  dreaded lash,
But they saw their well-loved mountains full in view,
And they charged beneath the stockwhip with a
  sharp and sudden dash,
And off into the mountain scrub they flew.

Then fast the horsemen followed, where the gorges
  deep and black

Resounded to the thunder of their tread,
And the stockwhips woke the echoes, and they
  fiercely answered back
From cliffs and crags that beetled overhead.
And upward, ever upward, the wild horses held
  their way,
Where mountain ash and kurrajong grew wide;
And the old man muttered fiercely, 'We may bid
  the mob good day,
No man can hold them down the other side.'

When they reached the mountain's summit, even
  Clancy took a pull –
It well might make the boldest hold their breath;
The wild hop scrub grew thickly, and the hidden
  ground was full
Of wombat holes, and any slip was death.
But the man from Snowy River let the pony have
  his head,
And he swung his stockwhip round and gave a
  cheer,
And he raced him down the mountain like a torrent
  down its bed,
While the others stood and watched in very fear.

He sent the flint stones flying, but the pony kept its
  feet,
He cleared the fallen timber in his stride,
And the man from Snowy River never shifted in his
  seat –
It was grand to see that mountain horseman ride.

Through the stringy-barks and saplings, on the rough
 and broken ground,
Down the hillside at a racing pace he went;
And he never drew the bridle till he landed safe
 and sound
At the bottom of that terrible descent.

He was right among the horses as they climbed the
 farther hill,
And the watchers on the mountain, standing mute,
Saw him ply the stockwhip fiercely; he was right
 among them still
As he raced across the clearing in pursuit.
Then they lost him for a moment, where two mountain
 gullies met
In the ranges – but a final glimpse reveals
On a dim and distant hillside the wild horses racing yet,
With the man from Snowy River at their heels.

And he ran them single-handed till their sides were
 white with foam;
He followed like a bloodhound on their track,
Till they halted, cowed and beaten; then he turned
 their heads for home,
And alone and unassisted brought them back.
But his hardy mountain pony he could scarcely raise
 a trot,
He was blood from hip to shoulder from the spur;
But his pluck was still undaunted, and his courage
 fiery hot,
For never yet was mountain horse a cur.

And down by Kosciusko, where the pine-clad ridges
  raise
Their torn and rugged battlements on high,
Where the air is clear as crystal, and the white stars
  fairly blaze
At midnight in the cold and frosty sky,
And where around the Overflow the reed-beds
  sweep and sway
To the breezes, and the rolling plains are wide,
The Man from Snowy River is a household world
  today,
And the stockmen tell the story of his ride.

A.B. ('Banjo') Paterson, 1864-1941

Jim's Whip

Yes, there it hangs upon the wall
And never gives a sound,
The hand that trimmed its greenhide fall
Is hidden undergound,
There, in that patch of sally shade,
Beneath that grassy mound.

I never take it from the wall,
That whip belonged to him,
The man I singled from them all,
He was my husband, Jim;
I see him now, so straight and tall,

So long and lithe of limb.

That whip was with him, night and day
When he was on the track;
I've often heard him laugh, and say
That when they heard its crack,
After the breaking of the drought,
The cattle all came back.

And all the time that Jim was here
A-working on the run
I'd hear that whip ring sharp and clear
Just about set of sun
To let me know that he was near
And that his work was done.

I was away that afternoon,
Penning the calves, when, bang!
I heard his whip, 'twas rather soon —
A thousand echoes rang
And died away among the hills,
As toward that hut I sprang.

I made the tea and waited but,
Seized by a sudden whim,
I went and sat outside the hut
Watching the light grow dim —
I waited there till after dark,
But not a sign of Jim.

The evening air was damp with dew;
Just as the clock struck ten

His horse came riderless – I knew
What was the matter then.
Why should the Lord have singled out
My Jim from other men?

I took the horse and found him where
He lay beneath the sky
With blood all clotted on his hair;
I felt too dazed to cry –
I held him to me as I prayed
To God that I may die.

But sometimes now I seem to hear –
Just when the air grows chill –
A single whip-crack, sharp and clear,
Re-echo from the hill.
That's Jim, to let me know he's near
And thinking of me still.

Barcroft Boake, 1866-1892

The Banks of the Condamine

Oh, hark the dogs are barking, love,
I can no longer stay,
The men are all gone mustering
And it is nearly day.
And I must off by the morning light
Before the sun doth shine,
To meet the Sydney shearers

On the banks of the Condamine.

O Willie, dearest Willie,
I'll go along with you,
I'll cut off all my auburn fringe
And be a shearer too,
I'll cook and count your tally, love,
While ringer-o you shine,
And I'll wash your greasy moleskins
On the banks of the Condamine.

Oh, Nancy, dearest Nancy,
With me you cannot go,
The squatters have given orders, love,
No woman should do so;
Your delicate constitution
Is not equal unto mine,
To stand the constant tigering
On the banks of the Condomine.

Oh, Nancy, dearest Nancy,
Please do not hold me back,
Down there the boys are waiting,
And I must be on the track;
So here's a good-bye kiss, love,
Back home here I'll incline
When we've shore the last of the jumbucks
On the banks of the Condamine.

Traditional

Ballad of the Drover

Across the stony ridges,
Across the rolling plain,
Young Harry Dale, the drover,
Comes riding home again.
And well his stock-horse bears him,
And light of heart is he,
And stoutly his old packhorse
Is trotting by his knee.

Up Queensland way with cattle
He's travelled regions vast,
And many months have vanished
Since home-folks saw him last.
He hums a song of someone
He hopes to marry soon;
And hobble-chains and camp-ware
Keep jingling to the tune.

Beyond the hazy dado
Against the lower skies
And yon blue line of ranges
The station homestead lies.
And thitherward the drover
Jogs through the hazy noon,
While hobble-chains and camp-ware
Are jingling to a tune.

An hour has filled the heavens
With storm-clouds inky black;

At times the lightning trickles
Around the drover's track;
But Harry pushes onward,
His horses' strength he tries,
In hope to reach the river
Before the flood shall rise.

The thunder, pealing o'er him,
Goes rumbling down the plain;
And sweet on thirsty pastures
Beats fast the crashing rain;
Then every creek and gully
Sends forth its tribute flood –
The river runs a banker
All stained with yellow mud.

Now Harry speaks to Rover,
The best dog on the plains,
And to his hardy horses,
And strokes their shaggy manes:
'We've breasted bigger rivers
When floods were at their height,
Nor shall this gutter stop us
From getting home tonight.'

The thunder growls a warning,
The blue, forked lightnings gleam;
The drover turns his horses
To swim the fatal stream.
But, oh! the flood runs stronger
Than e'er it ran before;

Than e'er it ran before;
The saddle-horse is failing
And only half-way o'er!

When flashes next the lightning
The flood's grey breast is blank;
A cattle-dog and packhorse
Are struggling up the bank,
But in the lonely homestead
The girl shall wait in vain –
He'll never pass the stations
In charge of stock again.

The faithful dog a moment
Lies panting on the bank,
Then plunges through the current
To where his master sank.
And round and round in circles
He fights with failing strength,
Till, gripped by wilder waters,
He fails and sinks at length.

Across the flooded lowlands
And slopes of sodden loam
The packhorse struggles bravely
To take dumb tidings home;
And mud-stained, wet, and weary,
He goes by rock and tree,
With clanging chains and tinware
All sounding eerily.

Henry Lawson, 1867-1922

A Bush Christening

On the outer Barcoo, where the churches are few,
And men of religion are scanty,
On a road never cross'd,'cept by folks that are lost,
One Michael Magee had a shanty.

Now this Mike was the dad of a ten-year-old lad,
Plump, healthy, and stoutly conditioned;
He was strong as the best, but poor Mike had no rest
For the youngster had never been christened.

And his wife used to cry, 'If the darlin' should die
Saint Peter would not recognise him.'
But by luck he survived till a preacher arrived,
Who agreed straightaway to baptise him.

Now the artful young rogue, while they held their
   collogue,
With his ear to the keyhole was listenin'
And he muttered in fright, while his features turned
   white,
'What the devil and all is this christenin'?'

He was none of your dolts – he had seen them
   brand colts,
And it seemed to his small understanding,
If the man in the frock made him one of the flock,
It must mean something like branding.

So away with a rush he set off for the bush,
While the tears in his eyelids they glistened –

''Tis outrageous,' says he, 'to brand youngsters
  like me,
I'll be dashed if I'll stop to be christened.'

Like a young native dog he ran into a log,
And his father with language uncivil,
Never heeding the 'praste', cried aloud in his haste,
'Come out and be christened, you divil!'

But he lay there as snug as a bug in a rug,
And his parents in vain might reprove him,
Till His Reverence spoke (he was fond of a joke)
'I've a notion,' says he, 'that'll move him.

'Poke a stick up the log, give the spalpeen a prog;
Poke him aisy – don't hurt him or maim him;
'Tis not long that he'll stand, I've the water at hand,
As he rushes out this end I'll name him.

'Here he comes, and for shame! ye've forgotten
  the name –
Is it Patsy or Michael of Dinnis?'
Here the youngster ran out, and the priest gave
  a shout –
'Take your chance, wid "Maginnis"!'

As the howling young cub ran away to the scrub
Where he knew that pursuit would be risky,
The priest, as he fled, flung a flask at his head
That was labelled 'Maginnis's Whisky!'

And Maginnis Magee has been made a J.P.,

And the one thing he hates more than sin is
To be asked by the folk, who have heard of the joke,
How he came to be christened Maginnis!

A.B. ('Banjo') Paterson, 1864-1941

The Squatter's Man

Come all ye lads an' list to me,
That's left your homes an' crossed the sea,
To try your fortune, bound or free,
  All in this golden land.
For twelve long months I had to pace,
Humping my swag with a cadging face,
Sleeping in the bush, like the sable race,
As in my song you'll understand.

Unto this country I did come,
A regular out-and-out new chum.
I then abhorred the sight of rum –
  Teetotal was my plan.
But soon I learned to wet one eye –
Misfortune oft-times made me sigh.
To raise fresh funds I was forced to fly,
And be a squatter's man.

Soon at the station I appeared,
I saw the squatter with his beard,
And up to him I boldly steered

With my swag and billy-can.
I said 'Kind sir, I want a job!'
Said he, 'Do you know how to snob,
Or can you break a bucking cob?'
Whilst my figure he did scan.

''Tis now I want a useful cove
To stop at home and not to rove.
The scamps go about – a regular drove –
  I suppose you're one of the clan?
But I'll give you ten bob, ten, sugar and tea:
And very soon I hope you'll be
A handy squatter's man.

'At daylight you must milk the cows,
Make butter, cheese, an' feed the sows,
Put on the kettle, the cook arouse,
  And clean the family shoes.
The stable an' sheep yard clean out,
And always answer when we shout,
With "Yes, ma'm, and No, sir," mind your mouth,
And my youngsters don't abuse.

'You must fetch wood an' water, bake an' boil.
Act as butcher when we kill;
The corn an' taters you must hill,
  Keep the garden spick and span.
You must not scruple in the rain
To take to market all the grain.
Be sure you come sober back again
To be a squatter's man.'

He sent me to an old bark hut,
Inhabited by a greyhound slut,
Who put her fangs in my poor fut,
And snarling, off she ran.
So once more I'm looking for a job,
Without a copper in my fob.
Wiith Ben Hall or Gardiner I'd rather job
Than be a squatter's man.

Anonymous

The Geebung Polo Club

It was somewhere up the country, in a land of rock
and scrub,
That they formed an institution called the Geebung
Polo Club.
They were long and wiry natives from the rugged
mountainside,
And the horse was never saddled that the Geebungs
couldn't ride;
But their style of playing polo was irregular and
rash –
They had mighty little science, but a mighty lot of
dash:
And they played on mountain ponies that were
muscular and strong,
Though their coats were quite unpolished, and their
manes and tails were long.

And they used to train those ponies wheeling cattle
in the scrub;
They were demons, were the members of the
Geebung Polo Club.

It was somewhere up the country, in a city's smoke
and steam,
That a polo club existed, called the 'Cuff and Collar
Team'.
As a social institution 'twas a marvellous success,
For the members were distinguished by exclusiveness
and dress.
They had natty little ponies that were nice, and
smooth, and sleek,
For their cultivated owners only rode 'em once a
week.
So they started up the country in pursuit of sport and
fame.
For they meant to show the Geebungs how they
ought to play the game;
And they took their valets with them – just to give
their boots a rub
Ere they started operations on the Geebung Polo
Club.

Now my readers can imagine how the contest ebbed
and flowed,
When the Geebung boys got going it was time to
clear the road;
And the game was so terrific that ere half the time
was gone

A spectator's leg was broken – just from merely
  looking on.
For they waddied one another till the plain was
  strewn with dead,
While the score was kept so even that they neither
  got ahead.
And the Cuff and Collar Captain, when he tumbled
  off to die
Was the last surviving player – so the game was
  called a tie.
Then the Captain of the Geebungs raised him slowly
  from the ground,
Though his wounds were mostly mortal, yet he
  fiercely gazed around;
There was no one to oppose him – all the rest were
  in a trance.
So he scrambled on his pony for his last expiring
  chance.
For he meant to make an effort to get the victory to
  his side:
So he struck at goal – and missed it – then tumbled
  off and died.

By the old Campaspe River, where the breezes shake
  the grass,
There's a row of little gravestones that the stockmen
  never pass,
For they bear a rude inscription saying, 'Stranger,
  drop a tear,
For the Cuff and Collar players and the Geebung
  boys lie here.'

And on misty moonlit evenings, while the dingoes
  howl around,
You can see their shadows flitting down the phantom
  polo ground;
You can hear the loud collisions as the flying players
  meet,
And the rattle of the mallets, and the rush of ponies'
  feet,
Till the terrified spectator rides like blazes to the
  pub –
He's been haunted by the spectres of the Geebung
  Polo Club.

A.B. ('Banjo') Paterson, 1864-1941

The Mailboy's Ride

He rode from Port Bowen bravely,
With his life held in his hands,
To carry the mail to safety
Across the wide burning sands.

Brave men who carried before him,
Blacks killed in the timber's shade;
At the first camp of the mailman,
Four graves show where they laid.

'Twas death not to reach the camp place
Ere darkness grew o'er the land,
For there had the only water

Been found on those plains of sand.

He reached the first camp in safety,
No sign of the blacks about,
So when he had eaten his supper
He tethered his horses out.

He lay down to rest in the shelter,
But long ere the break of day
He saddled his hack and pack-horse
And started once more away.

'I think I will have a smoko,'
He said, and he slackened rein,
But his horse plunged madly forward,
And he fell with a cry of pain.

He knew that his leg was broken,
And a sharp pain in his side
Told that his ribs were injured
With sixty miles to ride.

Alone on that awful desert
No hope of succour near,
He cried to God in heaven
As he fought with the rising fear.

'Oh God, Thou hast helped Thy children
Through dangers in days gone past;
Thou knowest that on this desert
Wounded and lone I'm cast.

'And now in my time of trouble,
To whom can I turn but Thee
Who rulest the earth and heavens,
The wind and the raging sea.

'Oh God of my fathers help me,'
He cried as he crawled in pain
To where the horses stood waiting,
And caught up the hanging rein.

Then slowly, with painful effort,
He mounted and rode away,
For he knew that within an hour
Would commence another day.

On as the morning brightened
He rode and he rode for life,
For over his aching body
Weakness and pain held strife.

On till the evening shadows
Steadied his fevered brain,
And in the darkness before him
A bright light shone on the plain.

The men at the station waiting
Cheered as they heard him come,
But the figure that stopped before them
Struck even the roughest dumb.

Then tenderly, kind as women,
They lifted the drooping lad,

With eyes closed tight, white faces,
And hearts all at once grown sad.

And through long weeks of fever
They watched by the sick boy's side,
And in his fevered ramblings
He told of that awful ride.

At night round the pleasant campfire
Those men still tell the tale
How across the Australian desert
The boy brought the Royal Mail.

Anonymous

The Man from Ironbark

It was the man from Ironbark who struck the Sydney
town,
He wandered over street and park, he wandered up
and down,
He loitered here, he loitered there, till he was like to
drop,
Until at last in sheer despair he sought a barber's
shop.
''Ere! shave my beard and whiskers off, I'll be a man
of mark,
I'll go and do the Sydney toff up home in Ironbark,'

The barber man was small and flash, as barbers
mostly are,
He wore a strike-your-fancy sash, he smoked a huge
cigar:
He was a humorist of note and keen at repartee,
He laid the odds and kept a 'tote', whatever that may
be,
And when he saw our friend arrive, he whispered
'Here's a lark!'
Just watch me catch him all alive, this man from
Ironbark.'

There were some gilded youths that sat along the
barber's wall.
Their eyes were dull, their heads were flat, they had
no brains at all;
To them the barber passed the wink, his dexter eye
lid shut,

'I'll make this bloomin' yokel think his bloomin'
   throat is cut.'
And as he soaped and rubbed it in he made a rude
   remark;
'I s'pose the flats is pretty green up there in
   Ironbark.'

A grunt was all reply he got; he shaved the
   bushman's chin,
Then made the water boiling hot and dipped the
   razor in.
He raised his hand, his brow grew black, he paused
   a while to gloat,
Then slashed the red-hot razor-back across his
   victim's throat;
Upon the newly-shaven skin it made a livid mark –
No doubt it fairly took him in – the man from
   Ironbark.

He fetched a wild up-country yell, might wake the
   dead to hear,
And though his throat, he knew full well, was cut
   from ear to ear,
He struggled gamely to his feet, and faced the
   murderous foe;
'You've done for me! you dog, I'm beat! One hit
   before I go,
I only wish I had a knife, you blessed murderous
   shark,
But you'll remember all your life the man from
   Ironbark.'

A peeler who heard the din came in to see the show;
He tried to run the bushman in, but he refused to go.
And when at last the barber spoke, and said, ''Twas
   all in fun –
'Twas just a little harmless joke, a trifle overdone.'
'A joke!' he cried. 'By George, that's fine; a lively sort
   of lark;
I'd like to catch that murdering swine some night in
   Ironbark.'

And now while round the shearing floor the listening
   shearers gape,
He tells the story o'er and o'er, and brags of his
   escape.
'Them barber chaps what keeps a tote, by George,
   I've had enough,
One tried to cut my bloomin' throat, but thank the
   Lord it's tough.'
And whether he's believed or not, there's one thing
   to remark,
That flowing beards are all the go way up in
   Ironbark.

A.B. ('Banjo') Paterson, 1864-1941

The Overlander

There's a trade you all know well –
It's bringing cattle over –
I'll tell about the time
When I became a drover.
I made up my mind to try the spec,
To the Clarence I did wander,
And brought a mob of duffers there
To begin as an overlander.

Chorus:
Pass the wine round, boys
Don't let the bottle stand there,
For tonight we'll drink the health
Of every overlander.

When the cattle were all mustered,
And the outfit ready to start,
I saw the lads all mounted,
With their swags left in the cart.
All kinds of men I had
From France, Germany and Flanders;
Lawyers, doctors, good and bad,
In the mob of overlanders.

From the road I then fed out
Where the grass was green and young;
When a squatter with curse and shout
Told me to move along.
I said, 'You're very hard;

Take care, don't raise my dander,
For I'm a regular knowing card
The Queensland overlander.'

'Tis true we pay no licence,
And our run is rather large;
'Tis not often they can catch us,
So they cannot make a charge.
They think we live on store beef,
But no, I'm not a gander;
When a good fat stranger joins the mob,
'He'll do,' says the overlander.

Traditional

The Kelly Gang

Oh, Paddy dear, and did you hear
The news that's going round,
On the head of bold Ned Kelly
They have placed two thousand pound.
And on Steve Hart, Joe Byrne and Dan,
Two thousand more they'd give,
But if the price was doubled boys,
The Kelly Gang would live.

'Tis hard to think such plucky hearts
In crime should be employed,
'Tis by police persecution
They have been much annoyed.
Revenge is sweet, and in the bush
They can defy the law,
Such sticking up and plundering
You never saw before.

'Twas in November, Seventy-eight,
When the Kelly Gang came down,
Just after shooting Kennedy,
To famed Euroa town;
To rob the bank of all its gold
Was their idea that day,
Blood-horses they were mounted on
To make their getaway.

So Kelly marched into the bank,
A cheque all in his hand,

For to have it changed to money
Of Scott he did demand.
And when that he refused him,
He, looking at him straight,
Said, 'See here, my name's Ned Kelly,
And this here man's my mate.'

With pistols pointed at his nut,
Poor Scott did stand amazed,
His stick he would have like to cut,
But he was with funk half crazed;
The poor cashier, with real fear,
Stood trembling at the knees,
But at last they both saw 'twas no use
And handed out the keys.

The safe was quickly gutted then,
The drawers turned out as well,
The Kellys being quite polite,
Like any noble swell.
With flimsies, gold and silver coin,
The threepennies and all
Amounting to two thousand pounds,
They made a glorious haul.

'Now hand out all your firearms,'
The robber boldly said,
'And all your ammunition –
Or a bullet through your head.
Now get your wife and children –
Come, man, look alive;

All jump into this buggy
And we'll take you for a drive.'

They took them to a station
About three miles away,
And kept them close imprisoned
Until the following day.
The owner of the station
And those in his employ
And a few unwary travellers
Their company did enjoy.

An Indian hawker fell in too,
As everybody knows,
He came in handy to the gang
By fitting them with clothes.
Then with their worn-out clothing
They made a few bonfires,
And then destroyed the telegraph
By cutting down the wires.

Oh, Paddy dear, do shed a tear,
I can't but sympathise,
Those Kellys are the devils,
For they've made another rise;
This time across the billabong,
On Morgan's ancient beast,
They've robbed the banks of thousands
And in safety did retreat.

The matter may be serious, Pat,
But still I can't but laugh,

To think the tales the bobbies told
Must all amount to chaff.
They said they had them hemmed in,
They could not get away,
But they turned up in New South Wales,
And made the journey pay.

They rode into Jerilderie town
At twelve o'clock at night,
Aroused the troopers from their beds,
And gave them an awful fright,
They took them in their night-shirts,
Ashamed I am to tell,
Then covered them with revolvers
And locked them in a cell.

Next morning being Sunday morn
Of course they must be good,
They dressed themselves in troopers' clothes,
And Ned, he chopped some wood.
No one there suspected them,
As troopers they did pass,
And Dan, the most religious one,
Took the sergeant's wife to Mass.

They spent the day most pleasantly,
Had plenty of good cheer,
Fried beefsteak and onions,
Tomato sauce and beer;
The ladies in attendance
Indulged in pleasant talk,

And just to ease the troopers' minds,
They took them for a walk.

On Monday morning early,
Still masters of the ground,
They took their horses to the forge
And had them shod all round;
Then back they came and mounted,
Their plans all laid so well,
In company with troopers,
They stuck up the Royal Hotel.

They bailed up all the occupants,
And placed them in a room,
Saying, 'Do as we command you,
Or death will be your doom,'
A Chinese cook, 'No savvy,' cried,
Not knowing what to fear,
But they brought him to his senses
With a lift under the ear.

All who now approached the house
Just shared a similar fate,
In hardly any time at all
The number was twenty-eight.
They shouted freely for all hands,
And paid for all they drank,
And two of them remained in charge,
And two went to the bank.

The farce was here repeated
As I've already told,

They bailed up all the banker's clerks
And robbed them of their gold.
The manager could not be found,
And Kelly, in great wrath,
Searched high and low and luckily
He found him in his bath.

The robbing o'er, they mounted then,
To make a quick retreat,
They swept away with all their loot
By Morgan's ancient beast;
And where they've gone I do not know,
If I did I wouldn't tell,
So now, until I hear from them,
I'll bid you all farewell.

Anonymous

The Fire at Ross's Farm

The squatter saw his pastures wide
  Decrease, as one by one
The farmers moving to the west
  Selected on his run;
Selectors took the water up
  And all the black-soil round;
The best grass-land the squatter had
  Was spoilt by Ross's ground.

Now many schemes to shift old Ross
  Had racked the squatter's brains,
But Sandy had the stubborn blood
  Of Scotland in his veins;
He held the land and fenced it in,
  He cleared and ploughed the soil,
And year by year a richer crop
  Repaid him for his toil.

Between the homes for many years
  The devil left his tracks:
The squatter 'pounded Ross's stock,
  And Sandy 'pounded Black's.
A well upon the lower run
  Was filled with earth and logs
And Black laid bait about the farm
  To poison Ross's dogs.

It was, indeed, a deadly feud
  Of class and creed and race
So Fate supplied a Romeo
  And a Juliet in the case;
And more than once across the flats,
  Beneath the Southern Cross,
Young Robert Black was seen to ride
  With pretty Jenny Ross.

One Christmas time, when months of drought
  Had parched the western creeks,
The bush-fires started to the north
  And travelled south for weeks.

At night along the river-side
  The scene was grand and strange –
The hill-fires looked like lighted streets
  Of cities in the range.

The cattle-tracks between the trees
  Were like long dusty aisles,
And on a sudden breeze the fire
  Would sweep along for miles;
Like sounds of distant musketry
  It crackled through the brakes,
And o'er the flat of silver grass
  It hissed like angry snakes.

It leapt across the flowing streams
  And raced the pastures through;
It climbed the trees, and lit the boughs,
  And fierce and fiercer grew.
The bees fell stifled in the smoke
  Or perished in their hives,
And with the stock the kangaroos
  Went flying for their lives.

The sun had set on Christmas Eve,
  When through the scrub-lands wide
Young Robert Black came riding home
  As only natives ride.
He galloped to the homestead door
  And gave the first alarm:
'The fire is past the granite spur,
  And close to Ross's farm.'

'Now, father, send the men at once,
　They won't be wanted here;
Poor Ross's wheat is all he has
　To pull him through the year.'
'Then let it burn,' the squatter said;
　'I'd like to see it done –
I'd bless the fire if it would clear
　Selectors from the run.

'Go if you will,' the squatter said,
　'You shall not take the men –
Go out and join your precious friends,
　But don't come here again.'
'I won't come back,' young Robert cried,
　And reckless in his ire,
He sharply turned the horse's head
　And galloped towards the fire.

And there for three long weary hours,
　Half-blind with smoke and heat,
Old Ross and Robert fought the flames
　That neared the ripened wheat.
The farmer's hand was nerved by fear
　Of danger and of loss;
And Robert fought the stubborn foe
　For love of Jenny Ross.

But serpent-like the curves and lines
　Slipped past them, and between
Until they reached the boundary where
　The old coach-road had been.
'The track is now our only hope.

There we must stand,' cried Ross.
'For naught on earth can stop the fire
    If once it gets across.'

Then came a cruel gust of wind,
    And, with a fiendish rush,
The flames leapt o'er the narrow path
    And lit the fence of brush.
'The crop must burn!' the farmer cried,
    'We cannot save it now,'
And down upon the blackened ground
    He dashed his ragged bough.

But wildly, in a rush of hope,
    His heart began to beat,
For o'er the cracking of the fire he heard
    The sound of horses' feet.
'Here's help at last,' young Robert cried,
    And even as he spoke
The squatter with a dozen men
    Came racing through the smoke.

Down on the ground the stockmen jumped
    And bared each brawny arm;
They tore green branches from the trees
    And fought for Ross's farm;
And when before the gallant band
    The beaten flames gave way
Two grimy hands in friendship joined –
    And it was Christmas Day.

Henry Lawson, 1867-1922

Farewell to Greta: A Ballad of Ned Kelly

Farewell my home in Greta,
My loved ones fare thee well;
It grieves my heart to leave you,
But here I must not dwell.
They placed a price upon my head,
My hands are stained with gore,
And I must roam the forest wild
Within the Australian shore.

But if they cross my cherished path
By all I hold on earth,
I'll give them cause to rue the day
Their mothers gave them birth.
I'll shoot them down like carrion crows
That roam our country wide,
And leave their bodies bleaching
Along some woodland side.

Oh Edward, darling brother,
Surely you would not go
So rashly to encounter
With such a mighty foe!
Now don't you know that Sydney
And Melbourne are combined,
And for your apprehension, Ned,
There are warrants duly signed?

To eastward lies great Bogong,

Towering to the sky,
From east to west and then you'll find
That's Gippsland lying by.
You know the country well, Ned,
So take your comrades there,
And profit by your knowledge of
The wombat and the bear.

And let no childish quarrelling
Cause trouble in the gang,
You're up with one another,
And guard my brother Dan.
See yonder ride four troopers,
One kiss before we part,
Now haste and join your comrades, Dan,
Joe Byrne and Stevey Hart.

Traditional

The Dying Stockman

A strapping young stockman lay dying,
His saddle supporting his head;
His two mates around him were crying
As he rose on his elbow and said:

Chorus:
'Wrap me up with my stockwhip and blanket,
And bury me deep down below,
Where the dingoes and crows can't molest me,

In the shade where the coolibahs grow.

'Oh had I the flight of the bronze-wing
Far o'er the plains I would fly,
Straight to the land of my childhood,
And there I would lay down and die.

'Then cut down a couple of saplings,
Place one at my head and my toe,
Carve on them cross, stockwhip and saddle,
To show there's a stockman below.

'Hark! There's a wail of a dingo
Watchful and weird – I must go,
For it tolls the death-knell of the stockman
From the gloom of the scrub below.

'There's tea in the battered old billy:
Place the pannikins all in a row.
And we'll drink to the next merry meeting,
In the place where all good fellows go.

'And oft in the shades of the twilight
When the soft winds are whispering low,
And the darkening shadows are falling,
Sometimes think of the stockman below.'

Traditional

Click Go the Shears

Out on the board the old shearer stands,
Grasping his shears in his long, bony hands,
Fixed is his gaze on the bare-bellied yeo,
Glory, if he gets her, won't he make the 'ringer' go!

Chorus:
Click go the shears, boys, click, click, click;
Wide is his blow and his hands move quick,
The ringer looks around and is beaten by a blow;
And curses the old snagger with the bare-bellied yeo.

In the middle of the floor, in his cane-bottomed chair
Is the boss of the board, with eyes everywhere;
Notes well each fleece as it comes to the screen,
Paying strict attention if it's taken off clean.

The colonial experience man, he is there, of course,
With his shiny leggins, just got off his horse;
Casting round his eye, like a real connoisseur,
Whistling the old tune, 'I'm the Perfect Lure.'

The tar-boy is there, awaiting in demand,
With his blackened tar-pot, and his tarry hand,
Sees one old sheep with a cut upon its back,
Here's what he's waiting for, 'Tar here, Jack.'

Shearing is all over and we've all got our cheques.
Roll up your swags, boys, we're off on the tracks;
The first pub we come to, it's there we'll have a
  spree,

And everyone that comes along, it's 'Have a drink
  with me!'

Down by the bar the old shearer stands,
Grasping his glass in his thin bony hands;
Fixed is his gaze on a green-painted keg,
Glory, he'll get down on it, ere he stirs a peg.

There we leave him standing, shouting for all hands,
Whilst all around him, every drinker stands;
His eyes are on the cask, which is now lowering fast.
He works hard, he drinks hard, and goes to hell at
  last!

Traditional

On Kiley's Run

The roving breezes come and go
  On Kiley's Run.
The sleepy river murmurs low,
And far away one dimly sees
Beyond the stretch of forest trees –
Beyond the foothills dusk and dun –
The ranges sleeping in the sun
  On Kiley's Run.

'Tis many years since first I came
  To Kiley's run,

More years than I would care to name
Since I, a stripling, used to ride
For miles and miles at Kiley's side,
The while in stirring tones he told
The stories of the days of old
  On Kiley's Run.

I see the old bush homestead now
  On Kiley's Run,
Just nestled down beneath the brow
Of one small ridge above the sweep
Of river flat, where willows weep
And jasmine flowers and roses bloom,
The air was laden with perfume
  On Kiley's Run.

We lived the good old station life
  On Kiley's Run,
With little thought of care or strife.
Old Kiley seldom used to roam,
He liked to make the Run his home,
The swagman never turned away
With empty hand at close of day
  From Kiley's Run.

We kept a racehorse now and then
  On Kiley's Run,
And neighb'ring stations brought their men
To meetings where the sport was free,
And dainty ladies came to see
Their champions ride; with laugh and song

The old house rang the whole night long
  On Kiley's Run.

The station hands were friends I wot
  On Kiley's Run,
A reckless, merry-hearted lot –
All splendid riders, and they knew
The 'boss' was kindness through and through.
Old Kiley always stood their friend,
And so they served him to the end
  On Kiley's Run.

But droughts and losses came apace
  To Kiley's Run,
Till ruin stared him in the face;
He toiled and toiled while lived the light,
He dreamed of overdrafts at night:
At length, because he could not pay,
His bankers took his stock away
  From Kiley's Run.

Old Kiley stood and saw them go
  From Kiley's Run.
The well-bred cattle marching slow;
His stockmen, mates for many a day,
They wrung his hand and went away.
Too old to make another start,
Old Kiley died – of broken heart,
  On Kiley's Run.

The owner lives in England now
  Of Kiley's Run.

He knows a racehorse from a cow;
But that is all he knows of stock:
His chiefest care is how to dock
Expenses, and he sends from town
To cut the shearers' wages down
　On Kiley's Run.

There are no neighbours anywhere
　Near Kiley's Run.
The hospitable homes are bare,
The gardens gone; for no pretence
Must hinder cutting down expense:
The homestead that we held so dear
Contains a half-paid overseer
　On Kiley's Run.

All life and sport and hope have died
　On Kiley's Run.
No longer there the stockmen ride;
For sour-faced boundary riders creep
On mongrel horses after sheep,
Through ranges where, at racing speed,
Old Kiley used to 'wheel the lead'
　On Kiley's Run.

There runs a lane for thirty miles
　Through Kiley's Run.
On either side the herbage smiles,
But wretched trav'lling sheep must pass
Without a drink or blade of grass
Thro' that long lane of death and shame:

The weary drovers curse the name
  Of Kiley's Run.

The name itself has changed of late
  Of Kiley's Run.
The call it 'Chandos Park Estate'.
The lonely swagman through the dark
Must hump his swag past Chandos Park.
The name is English, don't you see,
The old name sweeter sounds to me
  Of 'Kiley's Run'.

I cannot guess what fate will bring
  To Kiley's Run –
For chances come and changes ring –
I scarcely think 'twill always be
Locked up to suit an absentee;
And if he lets it out in farms
His tenants soon will carry arms
  On Kiley's Run.

A.B. ('Banjo') Paterson, 1864-1941

Billy Brink

There once was a shearer by the name of Bill Brink,
A devil for work and a devil for drink.
He'd shear two hundred a day without fear,
And he'd drink without stopping two gallons of beer.

When the pub opened up he was very first in
Roaring for whisky and howling for gin,
Saying, 'Jimmy, my boy, I'm dying of thirst,
Whatever you've got there just give to me first.'

Now Jimmy the barman who served him the rum
Hated the sight of old Billy the bum;
He came up too late, he came up too soon,
At morning, at evening, at night and at noon.

Now Jimmy the barman was cleaning the bar
With sulphuric acid locked in a jar.
He poured him a measure into a small glass,
Saying, 'After this drink you will surely say "Pass."'

'Well,' says Billy to Jimmy, 'the stuff tastes fine.
She's a new kind of liquor or whisky or wine.
Yes, that's the stuff, Jimmy, I'm strong as a Turk –
I'll break all the records today at my work.'

Well, all that day long there was Jim at the bar,
Too eager to argue, too anxious to fight,
Roaring and trembling with a terrible fear;
For he pictured the corpse of old Bill in his sight.

But early next morning there was Bill as before,
Roaring and bawling, and howling for more,
His eyeballs were singed and his whiskers deranged,
He had holes in his hide like a dog with the mange.

Said Billy to Jimmy, 'She sure was fine stuff,
It made me feel well but I ain't had enough.
It started me coughing, you know I'm no liar,
And every damn cough set my whiskers on fire!'

Traditional

Mulga Bill's Bicycle

'Twas Mulga Bill from Eaglehawk, that caught the
   cycling craze;
He turned away the good old horse that served him
   many days;
He dressed himself in cycling clothes, resplendent to
   be seen;
He hurried off to town and bought a shining new
   machine:
And as he wheeled it through the door, with air of
   lordly pride,
The grinning shop assistant said, 'Excuse me, can
   you ride?'

'See here, young man,' said Mulga Bill, 'from Walgett
   to the sea,
From Conroy's Gap to Castlereagh, there's none can
   ride like me.
I'm good all round at everything, as everybody
   knows,
Although I'm not the one to talk – I hate a man that
   blows.
But riding is my special gift, my chiefest, sole delight;

'Just ask a wild duck can it swim, a wild cat can it
   fight.
There's nothing clothed in hair or hide, or built of
   flesh or steel,

There's nothing walks or jumps or runs, on axle,
  hoof or wheel,
But what I'll sit, while hide will hold and girths and
  straps are tight;
I'll ride this here two-wheeled concern right away at
  sight.'

'Twas Mulga Bill, from Eaglehawk, that sought his
  own abode,
That perched above the Dead Man's Creek, beside
  the mountain road.
He turned the cycle down the hill and mounted for
  the fray,
But ere he'd gone a dozen yards it bolted clean
  away.
It left the track, and through the trees, just like a
silver streak,
It whistled down the awful slope, towards the Dead
  Man's Creek.

It shaved a stump by half an inch, it dodged a big
  white-box;
The very wallaroos in fright went scrambling up the
  rocks,
The wombats hiding in their caves dug deeper
  underground,
As Mulga Bill, as white as chalk, sat tight to every
  bound.
It struck a stone and gave a spring that cleared a
  fallen tree,
It raced beside a precipice as close as close could be;

And then as Mulga Bill let out one last despairing
  shriek
It made a leap of twenty feet into the Dead Man's
  Creek.

'Twas Mulga Bill, from Eaglehawk, that slowly swam
  ashore;
He said, 'I've had some narrer shaves and lively rides
  before;
I've rode a wild bull round a yard to win a five
  pound bet,
But this was the most awful ride that I've
  encountered yet.
I'll give that two-wheeled outlaw best; it's shaken all
  me nerve
To feel it whistle through the air and plunge and
  buck and swerve.
It's safe at rest in Dead Man's Creek we'll leave it
  lying still;
A horse's back is good enough henceforth for Mulga
  Bill.'

A.B. ('Banjo') Paterson, 1864-1941

Stir the Wallaby Stew

Poor Daddy's got five years or more,
As everybody knows;
And now he lives in Boggo Road,
Broad arrows on his clothes.
He branded all Brown's cleanskins,
And never left a trail,
So I'll relate the family's fate,
Since Daddy went to jail.

Chorus:
So stir the wallaby stew,
Make soup with the kangaroo's tail,
I tell you things are pretty crook
Since Dad got put in jail.

Our sheep all died a month ago,
Not rot, but flaming fluke.
Our cow got boozed last Christmas Day
With my big brother Luke;
And Mother has a shearer cove
Forever within hail,
The family will have grown a bit
When Dad gets out of jail.

Our Bess got shook upon a bloke,
He's gone we don't know where.
He used to act around the sheds,
But he ain't acted square.
I've sold the buggy on my own,

The place is up for sale.
That isn't all that won't be junked
When Dad gets out of jail.

They let Dad out before his time
To give us a surprise,
He came and looked around the place,
And gently damned our eyes.
He shook hands with the shearer cove,
And said he thought things stale,
So left him there to shepherd us,
And he battled back to jail.

Traditional

The Search

I've dropped me swag in many camps
From Queensland west to Boulder,
An' struck all sorts of outback champs
An' many a title-holder.
But though I've learned the episode
By drover told, an' dogger,
I've still to meet the bloke who rode
The big white bull through Wagga.

I struck the hero out at Hay
Who beat the red-back spider

In fourteen rounds one burnin' day;
An' up along the Gwydir
There lives the man outslept the toad –
A champeen blanket-flogger –
But he is not the bloke who rode
The big white bull through Wagga.

The cove that hung the Bogan Gate
Once called me in a hurry
To buy drinks for his 'China plate',
The bloke that dug the Murray.
An' though down south of Beechworth road
I met Big Bog the Frogger,
I've still to meet the bloke who rode
The big white bull through Wagga.

The man who steered the kangaroo
From Cue to Daly Waters;
The cove who raced the emu, too
To win three squatters' daughters;
I know the fellow moved the load
That stopped the Richmond logger;
But still I want the bloke that rode
The big white bull through Wagga.

But some fine day I'll run him down,
An' stop his flamin' skitin'.
I'll punch him on his lyin' crown,
Or go down gamely fightin'.
For *I'm* the bloke to who is owed
What's paid that limelight-hogger.

I'd *love* to meet that bloke who rode
The big white bull through Wagga.

Charles Shaw

The Old Bark Hut

In an old bark hut on the mountainside
In a spot that was lone and drear
A woman whose heart was aching sat
Watching from year to year.

A small boy, Jim, her only child,
Helped her to watch and wait
But the time never came when they could go free,
Free from the bond of hate.

For McConnel was out on the mountainside
Living without a hope
And seeing nothing before him now
But death by a hangman's rope.

Hated and chased by his fellow men,
To take him alive or dead;
An outlaw banned by the world was he,
With five hundred pounds on his head.

A message had come that evening which said
'Now Jim, you mustn't wait,

If you want to save your father, or
By heaven, you'll be too late.

'He's out at Mackinnon's Crossing, they say,
The track's rough, old man,
But if any here can do it – why
It's you and old Darky can.'

And Jim knew well what the message meant,
As he brought his horse to the door!
While away through the gathering darkness came
The sound of the river's roar.

But the brave little heart never faltered as
He stooped to kiss her goodbye
And said, 'God bless you, Mother dear,
I'll save Dad tonight or I'll die.'

The old horse answered the touch of his hand
And galloped away from the door;
He seemed to know 'twas a journey for life –
Well, he'd done such journeys before.

Out from the firelight, and through the rails,
Out through the ghastly trees,
While all the time the warning roar
Of the river came back on the breeze;

Steadily down the mountainside
He rode, for his course was plain,
Though his heart was heavy, though not with fear,
But because of that brand of Cain.

The boy thinks over his mother's last words:
'I'll love him as long as I live,
He must have time for repentance on earth
But surely God will forgive.'

As he glanced back over his shoulder there
She stood by the light of the door
Trying to pierce the darkness in vain,
Thinking she'd see him no more.

Then as he looked she bowed her head
And slowly turned away,
And the boy knew that the noble wife
Had knelt by the bed to pray.

Mile after mile, hour after hour,
And then just ahead, shining white,
Was the foam of Mackinnon's Crossing –
What a jump for old Darky tonight!

And then Jim thinks of the long, lone years
And the hopes that are crushed and dead;
And a woman whose heart is as true as steel,
As true as the day she was wed.

As she loved him then in the years gone by
When the future held promise in store,
So she loved him today when the future held
Nought but death by his country's law.

Jim pressed his knees to the saddle-flap
And tightened his hold on the rein;

They had jumped the river last summertime.
How he hoped they would do it again!

Then a voice rang out through the darkness there,
'Hold, now hold, stand still!
We know you, lad, it's too late to run;
Hands up or we'll shoot to kill.'

Then he knew that the police were around him,
In the darkness they moved to and fro;
For an instant he pulled on the bridle-rein,
But he promised his mother he'd go.

And he thought of the poor, sad woman alone,
Kneeling in prayer by the bed;
So he loosened the reins on old Darky's neck
And rushed at the river ahead.

Then a volley rang out through the forest dark –
A fall in the roaring flood;
And the darkness hid from all human eyes
The form that was stained with blood.

The horse struggled hard, the waters rushed on;
He sank to rise no more.
But the boy fought the flood in silence, inch
By inch to the other shore.

Slowly and sadly, but bravely on,
Brushing away the tears;
He was leaving behind in the river's flood
His friend and companion of years.

And all of the time the blood trickled down,
O God! what a hot, burning pain!
And he knew he was doing his duty clean;
He would never come back again.

Struggling on o'er the tough, dark track,
A horrible pain with each breath;
Till he came to the hut in the ranges
Where his father was hiding from death.

Staggering through the yielding door
Into the cold dark room
Where his father lay, and the faint firelight
Showed through the ghostly gloom.

The bushranger sprang up to his feet in alarm
And levelled the gun at his head
And his loud voice demanded, 'Who are you?
Speak quick, or you are dead.'

And then a weak little voice made answer,
'It's me; Mother sends you her love,
The police are back at the crossing now,
So clear out and meet Mother above.'

Then McConnel placed his gun by the wall
And knelt on the cold, hard floor;
And somehow the tears came rushing down
As they never had before.

His arms went round the brave little lad,
He nursed his head on his breast;

He seemed to know that the end was nigh
And Jim would soon be at rest.

And the boy was speaking feebly at last,
'They shot me back at the creek,
And old Darky is dead and gone, Dad,
And oh, I'm so tired and weak.'

Then his voice fell away in a whisper soft,
So faint it could scarcely be heard,
'Oh, Dad, clear out, they are coming fast;
Tell Mother I kept my word.'

Quickly in silence the police gathered round,
They had captured the beast in his lair,
The outlaw sat with the boy in his arms,
He seemed not to heed nor to care.

He was thinking now of the seed he had sown,
He was tasting its bitter fruit,
When the sergeant stepped to the door and said,
'McConnel, bail up, or I'll shoot.'

Then the sergeant placed a lamp by the door,
The rifles gleamed out in the light,
But the outlaw said, 'Sergeant O'Grady,
Let's have no more shooting tonight.

'You can take me now to the judgement seat
As God has taken this lad;
You'd die to take my life, you men –
He died to save his dad.

'I want you to help me to dig his grave,
And perhaps you will say a prayer;
Then you can take me and hang me dead –
It's my wife, or I wouldn't care.

'Carefully now . . . Oh, thank you, men,
Lay him as best you can;
The policeman is shown by his coat, of course,
But the tears – well, they show the man.

Then the party went back to the old bark hut
As the sun was mounting the hill;
No smoke arose from the chimney cold
And all was silent and still.

The sergeant opened the creaky door,
And lifted his cap with a start,
Ah, McConnel had broken the country's laws
And broken a woman's heart.

Anonymous

The Death of Halligan

Ho, men pile up the firewood
And let the cauldron boil
Whose bright contents will soon repay
The hardy miner's toil;
For yonder glittering treasure
Long weeks they've toiled below,
Then pile the faggots higher
And set them all aglow.

The fire is quickly kindled,
The flames leap up in sport,
And 'mid the red and lurid glare
Is seen the dark retort.
Right soon the work is finished,
The yellow gold is weighed,
It is the price for wretched souls
That Satan down hath paid.

Now Halligan has started
And left Rockhampton town
To visit the Alliance reef,
The gold to carry down.
To see him mount so stoutly
No human eye had guessed
That even now the shroud was drawn
High up upon his breast.

Alas, no dim presentiment

Passed through the rider's mind
That he would ne'er again behold
The home he left behind;
And as in pride of health and strength
He passed from out of door,
He little dreamed, as living man,
He'd enter there no more.

He got the gold, the cursed dross,
Through which he lost his life,
Through which his children orphans are
And widowed is his wife.
Then leaving Morinish behind,
To town he turned him back
And cantered speedily along
The old familiar track.

He came to where a darksome scrub
Extends along the road,
Where slimy frogs and crawling snakes
Take up their rank abode;
But far from noxious reptiles lurked
In yonder scrub that day,
Who with gloating eyes their victim watched
Come prancing on the way.

The pale assassins laid in wait
Behind a sheltering tree;
A shot was heard, the horseman reeled,
Then quickly turned to flee.
'Twas all too late, the ball had told,

His life-stream welled away,
And on the sod, a helpless clod,
The fated rider lay.

With crimsoned hands the felons clutched
The wages of their guilt;
Great heaven, to think for such a lure
His blood they foully spilt.
With blanching cheeks and trembling hearts
They anxious peered around,
Then took their ghastly burden up
And left the fatal ground.

What dastard fears were in their souls
Through all that frightful march,
Around them was the solemn bush,
Above the heavenly arch.
They only strove from human gaze
To screen their ruthless crime,
Nor cared that God's omniscient eye
Looked on them all the time.

Oh, how they started when a leaf
Was rustled by a bird,
How quailed their craven hearts when trees
The night-wind round them stirred.
And they rejoiced, I ween, to reach
That dark and swollen river,
Whose waves they fondly hoped would hide
The murdered man for ever.

And now their task was nearly done,

They stood upon the brink;
A sullen splash was faintly heard,
The corpse was seen to sink.
The eddies circled widely round
Where the pale stars seemed to quiver
And the blood-stained wretches turned in haste
And fled the darksome river.

But though, where scaly monsters roam
In yonder slimy bed
Poor Halligan, by murderous hand,
Had laid his gory head,
The swift Fitzroy refused to hold
The secret of his doom;
His corpse was found, in sacred ground
To find a Christian's tomb.

Now search, ye sharp detectives!
Hunt, bloodhounds of the law!
And from their sanguinary lairs
Those foul assassins draw;
And may their dreadful punishment
To all the world proclaim
That Queensland's justice will avenge
Such deeds of blood and shame.

Alexander Forbes, 1839-1879

The Wild Rover

Well, I've been a wild rover this many a year,
And I've spent all my money on whisky and beer.
But now I'm returning with gold in great store
And I never will play the wild rover no more;

Chorus
And it's no, nay, never,
No, nay, never, no more
Will I play the wild rover;
Nay, never no more

I went to a shanty I used to frequent
And I told the landlady my money was spent;
I asked her for credit, she answered me 'Nay!'
Such custom as yours I can get any day!'
Then I pulled from my pocket ten sovereigns bright
And the landlady's eyes opened wide with delight.
Said she, 'We have whisky and wines of the best
And the words that I told you were only in jest!'

There was Margaret and Kitty and Betsy and Sue,
And two or three more who belonged to our crew.
We'd sit up all night and make the place roar,
I've been a wild boy, but I'll be so no more.

And then as a prisoner to Cockatoo I was sent,
On a bed of cold straw for to lie and lament.
At last then I got what so long I'd looked for
And I never will play the wild rover no more.

I'll go home to my parents, confess what I've done,
And I'll ask them to pardon their prodigal son;
And if they will do so, as often before,
Then I never will play the wild rover no more.

Traditional

The Old Whim-horse

He's an old grey horse, with his head bowed sadly,
And with dim old eyes and a queer roll aft,
With the off-fore sprung and the hind screwed badly
And he bears all over the brands of graft;
And he lifts his head from the grass to wonder
Why by night and day now the whim is still,
Why the silence is, and the stampers' thunder
Sounds forth no more from the shattered mill.

In that whim he worked when the night-winds
  bellowed
On the riven summit of Giant's Hand,
And by day when prodigal Spring had yellowed
All the wide long sweep of enchanted land;
And he knew his shift, and the whistle's warning,
And he knew the calls of the boys below;
Through the years, unbidden, at night or morning,
He had taken his stand by the old whim bow.

But the whim stands still, and the wheeling swallow

In the silent shaft hangs her home of clay,
And the lizards flirt and the swift snakes follow
O'er the grass-grown brace in the summer day;
And the corn springs high in the cracks and corners
Of the forge, and down where the timber lies;
And the crows are perched like a band of mourners
On the broken hut on the Hermit's Rise.

All the hands have gone, for the rich reef paid out,
And the company waits till the calls come in;
But the old grey horse, like the claim, is played out,
And no market's near for his bones and skin.
So they let him live, and they left him grazing
By the creek, and oft in the evening dim
I have seen him stand on the rises, gazing
At the ruined brace and the rotting whim.

The floods rush high in the gully under,
And the lightnings lash at the shrinking trees,
Or the cattle down from the ranges blunder
As the fires drive by on the summer breeze.
Still the feeble horse at the right hour wanders
To the lonely ring, though the whistle's dumb,
And with hanging head by the bow he ponders
Where the whim-boy's gone – why the shifts don't
  come.

But there come a night when he sees lights glowing
In the roofless huts and the ravaged mill,
When he hears again the stampers going
Though the huts are dark and the stampers still:

When he sees the stream to the black roof clinging
As its shadows roll on the silver sands,
And he knows the voice of his driver singing,
And the knocker's clang where the braceman stands.

See the old horse take, like a creature dreaming,
On the ring once more his accustomed place;
But the moonbeams full on the ruins streaming
Show the scattered timbers and grass-grown brace.
Yet he hears the sled in the smithy falling
And the empty truck as it rattles back,
And the boy who stands by the anvil, calling:
And he turns and backs, and he takes up slack.

While the old drum creaks, and the shadows shiver
As the wind sweeps by and the hut doors close,
And the bats dip down in the shaft or quiver
In the ghostly light, round the grey horse goes;
And he feels the strain on his untouched shoulder,
Hears again the voice that was dear to him,
Sees the form he knew – and his heart grows bolder
As he works his shift by the broken whim.

He hears in the sluices the water rushing
As the buckets drain and the doors fall back:
When the early dawn in the east is blushing,
He is limping still round the old, old track.
Now he pricks his ears, with a neigh replying
To a call unspoken, with eyes aglow,
And he sways and sinks in the circle, dying;
From the ring no more will the grey horse go.

In a gully green, where a dam lies gleaming,
And the bush creeps back on a worked-out claim,
And the sleepy crows in the sun sit dreaming
On the timbers grey and a charred hut frame,
Where the legs slant down, and the hare is squatting
In the high rank grass by the dried-up course,
Nigh a shattered drum and king-post rotting
Are the bleached bones of the old grey horse.

Edward Dyson, 1865-1931

Corney's Hut

Old Corney built in Deadman's Gap,
A hut, where mountain shades grow denser,
And there he lived for many years,
A timber-getter and a fencer.
And no one knew if he'd a soul
Above long sprees or split-rail fences,
Unless, indeed, it was his dog
Who always kept his confidences.

There was a saw-pit in the range,
'Twas owned by three, and they were brothers
And visitors to Corney's hut –
'Twas seldom visited by others.
They came because, as they averred,
'Old Corney licked a gent infernal';

'His yarns,' if I might trust their word,
'Would make the fortune of a journal.'

In short, the splitter was a 'cure'
Who brightened up their lives' dull courses
And so on Sunday afternoons,
At Corney's hut they'd hang their horses.
They'd have a game of cards and smoke
And sometimes sing, which was a rum thing –
Unless, in spite of legal folk,
The splitter kept a drop of something.

If, as 'twas said, he was a swell
Before he sought these sombre ranges,
'Twixt mother's arms and coffin gear
He must have seen a world of changes.
But from his lips would never fall
A hint of home, or friends, or brothers,
And if he told his tale at all,
He must have told it as another's.

Though he was good at telling yarns,
At listening he excelled not less so,
And greatly helped the bushman's tales
With 'Yes,' 'Exactly so,' or 'Jes so.'
In short the hut became a club
Like our Assembly Legislative
Combining smokeroom hall, and pub,
Political and recreative.

Old Corney lived and Corney died,
As we will, too, on some tomorrow,

But not as Corney died, we hope,
Of heart-disease, and rum, and sorrow.
(We hope to lead a married life,
At times the cup of comfort quaffing;
And when we leave this world of strife
We trust that we may die of laughing.)

On New Year's Eve they found him dead –
For rum had made his life unstable –
They found him stretched upon his bed,
And also found, upon the table,
The coloured portrait of a girl –
Blue eyes of course. The hair was golden,
A faded letter and a curl,
And – well, we said the theme was olden.

The splitter had for days been dead
And cold before the sawyers found him,
And none had witnessed how he died
Except the dog who whimpered round him;
A noble friend, and of a kind
Who stays when other friends forsake us,
And he at last was left behind
To greet the rough bush undertakers.

This was a season when the bush
Was somewhat ruled by time and distance,
And bushmen came and tried the world,
And 'gave it best' without assistance.
Then one might die of heart-disease
And still be spared the inquest horrors,

And when the splitter laid at ease
So, also, did his sins and sorrows.

'Ole Corney's dead,' the bushmen said;
'He's gone at last, an' ne'er a blunder.'
And so they brought a horse and dray
And tools to 'tuck the old cove under',
The funeral wended through the range
And slowly round its rugged corners;
The reader will not think it strange
That Corney's dog was chief of mourners.

He must have thought the bushmen hard
And of his misery unheeding,
Because they shunned his anxious eyes
That seemed for explanation pleading.
At intervals his tongue would wipe
The jaws that seemed with anguish quaking;
As some strong hand impatiently
Might chide the tears for prison breaking.

They reached the rugged ways at last
A desolate bush cemetery,
Where now (our tale is of the past),
A thriving town its dead doth bury,
And where the bones of pioneers
Are found and thrown aside unheeded –
For later sleepers, blessed with tears
Of many friends, the graves are needed.

The funeral reached the bushmen's graves,
Where these old pioneers were sleeping,

And now while down the granite ridge
The shadow of the peak was creeping,
They dug a grave beneath the gum
And lowered the dead as gently as may be
As Corney's mother long before
Had laid him down to 'hush-a-baby'.

A bushman read the words to which
The others reverently listened,
Some bearded lips were seen to twitch,
Some shaded eyes with moisture glistened.
The boys had brought the splitter's tools,
And now they split and put together
Four panels such as Corney made,
To stand the stress of western weather.

'Old Corney's dead, he paid his bills,'
(These words upon the tree were graven),
'And oft a swagman down in luck
At Corney's mansion found a haven.'
But now the bushmen hurried on,
Lest darkness in the range should find them;
And strange to say they never saw
That Corney's dog had stayed behind them.

If one had thrown a backward glance
Along the rugged path that wended,
He might have seen a darker form
Upon the damp cold mound extended.
But soon their forms had vanished all,
And night came down the ranges faster,

And no one saw the shadows fall
Upon the dog that mourned his master.

Anonymous

Widgeegoara Joe

I'm only a backblock shearer, as clearly can be seen,
I've shorn in most of the famous sheds
On the plains of the Riverine;
I've shorn at most of the famous sheds,
And I've seen big tallies done.
But somehow or other, I don't know why,
I never became a gun.

Chorus
Hooray me boys, me shears are set,
And I feel both fit and well;
Tomorrow you'll see me at my pen
When the gaffer rings the bell.
With Hayden's Patent Thumb guards fixed,
And both my blades pulled back,
Away I'll go with my sardine blow,
For a century or the sack!

I've opened up the wind-pipe straight,
I've opened behind the ear,
I've shorn in all the possible styles in which

A man can shear.
I've studied all the strokes and blows
Of the famous men I've met,
But I've never succeeded in plastering up
Those three little figures yet.

When the boss walked onto the board today,
He stopped and stared at me,
For I'd mastered Moran's great shoulder-cut
As he could plainly see.
And when he comes round tomorrow, me boys,
I'll give his nerves a shock.
When he discovers that I have mastered
Pierce's Rangtang Block.

And if I succeed as I hope to do,
Then I intend to shear
At the Wagga demonstration,
That's held there every year.
It's there I'll lower the colours,
The colours of Mitchell and Co.,
Instead of Denning you will hear
Of Widgeegoara Joe.

Traditional

The Grass Stealers

In Australia where the cattle tracks
Are two miles wide,
And run from northern Queensland
To the Great Divide,
The drover and the shearer
And the rouseabouts, alas!
They wouldn't steal a penny,
But they all steal grass.

For the neddies never wander
If the going's good and sweet,
But stick around the fire
With the hobbles on their feet.
So Alf and Bill and Bendigo
And Harry of the Pass,
They wouldn't steal a copper,
But they all steal grass.

When the overlanders gather
In the wide and dusty plain,
When tomorrow's never mentioned,
And they never speak of rain,
When the blazing sun is setting
Like a disc of shining brass,
They wouldn't steal a copper,
But they all steal grass.

They steal it from the squatter;

They steal it from his run.
They steal it from the cocky
And think it mighty fun.
They steal if from each other,
And nothing can surpass
The methods of the travellers
Who all steal grass.

It's sundown on the Darling,
There's water in the bend,
But not a blade of forage
Where the cattle musters end.
And let the horses pass!
So it's nip the squatter's wire
They'll take the track tomorrow
With their bellies full of grass.

Now stealing grass for horses
May be a horrid crime,
Especially to the squatter
With his paddocks lush and prime;
But a man who wouldn't steal
A bit of grass to feed his horse
Should be flung into the Darling
Or some other watercourse.

J. Murray Allison, 1879-1929

The Ryebuck Shearer

Well, I come from the south and my name is Field
And when my shears are properly steeled,
It's a hundred or more I have very often peeled
And of course I'm a ryebuck shearer.

Chorus:
If I don't shear a tally before I go
My shears and stones in the river I'll throw,
And I'll never open Sawbees or take another blow,
Till I prove I'm a ryebuck shearer.

There's a bloke on the board and I heard him say
That I couldn't shear a hundred sheep a day,
But one fine day, mate, I'll show him the way
I'll prove I'm a ryebuck shearer.

You ought to see our ringer, he's nothing but a farce
When the cobbler's coming up, he's always first
  to pass,
As for the shearing, he's more ass than class
And he'll never be a ryebuck shearer.

There's a swaggie down the creek, his name is Jack,
He rolled into town with a swag on his back;
He asked us for a job, said he needed a few bob
And he swears he's a ryebuck shearer.

Yes, I'll make a splash, and I won't say when,
I'll up off me arse and I'll into the pen

While the ringer's shearing eight, mate, I'll be
  shearing ten
And I'll prove I'm a ryebuck shearer.

Traditional

How the Sailor Rode the Brumby

There was an agile sailor lad
Who longed to know the bush
So with his swag and billycan
He said he'd make a push.
He left his ship in Moreton Bay
And faced the Western run,
And asked his way, ten times a day,
And steered for Bandy's Run.

Said Bandy: 'You can start, my son,
If you can ride a horse,'
For stockmen on the cattle-run
Were wanted there, of course.
Now Jack had strode the cross-bars oft
On many a bounding sea,
So reckoned he'd be safe enough
On any moke you see.

They caught him one and saddled it,
And led it from the yard,

It champed a bit and sidled round
And at the sailor sparred.
Jack towed her to him with a grin,
He eyed her fore and aft;
Then thrust his foot the gangway in
And swung aboard the craft.

The watchers tumbled off the rail,
The boss lay down and roared,
While Jack held tight by mane and tail
And rocked about on board.
But still he clung as monkeys cling
To rudder, line and flap,
Although at every bound and spring
They thought his neck must snap.

They stared to see him stick aloft
The brum bucked fierce and free,
But he had strode the cross-bars oft
On many a rolling sea.
The saddle from the rolling back
Went spinning in mid-air,
Whilst two big boots were flung off Jack
And four shoes off the mare.

The bridle broke and left her free,
He grasped her round the neck;
'We're 'mong the breakers now,' cried he,
'There's bound to be a wreck,'
The brumby struck and snorted loud,
She reared and pawed the air,

It was the grandest sight the crowd
Had ever witnessed there.

For Jack with arms and legs held tight
The brumby's neck hung round
And yelled, 'A pilot, quick as light,
Or strike me I'm aground.'
The whites and blacks climbed on the rails,
The boss stood smiling by
As Jack exclaimed, 'Away the sails!'
The brum began to fly.

She bounded first against the gate,
And Jack cried out, 'Astern!'
Then struck a whirlpool – at any rate
That was the sailor's yarn.
The brumby spun him round and round,
She reared and kicked and struck
And with alternate bump and bound
In earnest began to buck.

A tree loomed on the starboard bow,
And 'Port your helm!' cried he;
She fouled a bush and he roared 'You scow!'
And 'Keep to the open sea!'
From ear to tail he rode her hard,
From tail to ears again,
One mile beyond the cattle yard
And back across the plain.

Now high upon the pommel bumped,
Now clinging on the side,

And on behind the saddle lumped
With arms and legs flung wide,
They only laughed the louder then
When the mare began to back
Until she struck the fence at last
Then sat and looked at Jack.

He gasped, 'I'm safe in port at last,
I'll quit your bounding mane!'
Dropped off and sang, 'All danger's passed
And Jack's come home again.'
Old Jack has been a stockman now
On Bandy's farm for years
Yet memories of that morning's fun
To many still bring tears.

Anonymous

Carbine's Great Victory in the Melbourne Cup, 1890

The race is run, the Cup is won,
The great event is o'er.
The grandest horse that strode a course
Has led them home once more.

I watched with pride your sweeping stride
Before you ranged in line,

For far and near a ringing cheer
Was echoed for Carbine.

The start was made, no time delayed,
Before they got away,
Those horses great, some thirty-eight,
All eager for the fray.

No better start could human heart
To sportsmen ever show
As Watson did, each jockey bid
Get ready for to go.

With lightning speed, each gallant steed
Along the green sward tore;
Each jockey knew what he must do
To finish in the fore.

But Ramage knew his mount was true
Though he had 10-5 up,
For Musket's son had great deeds done
Before that Melbourne Cup.

No whip, nor spur, he needs to stir
A horse to greater speed;
He knew as well as man can tell
When he could take the lead.

So on he glides with even strides,
Though he is led by nine;
But Ramage knows before they close
He'll try them with Carbine.

The bend is passed; the straight at last:
He takes him to the fore.
The surging crowd with voices loud
The stud's name loudly roar.

The jockey too, he full well knew
The race was nearly o'er,
As to his mane he slacked the rein:
No need to urge him more.

Brave horse and man who led the van
On that November day!
Your records will be history still
When ye have passed away.

For such a race, for weight and pace,
Has never been put up
As that deed done by Musket's son
In the 1890 Cup.

Anonymous

Holy Dan

It was in the Queensland drought;
And over hill and dell,
No grass – the water far apart,
All dry and hot as hell.

The wretched bullock teams drew up
Beside a water-hole –
They'd struggled though dust and drought
For days to reach this goal.

And though the water rendered forth
A rank, unholy stench,
The bullocks and the bullockies
Drank deep their thirst to quench.

Two of the drivers cursed and swore
As only drivers can.
The other one, named Daniel,
Best known as Holy Dan,
Admonished them and said it was
The Lord's all-wise decree;
And if they'd only watch and wait,
A change they'd quickly see.

'Twas strange that of Dan's bullocks
Not one had gone aloft,
But this, he said, was due to prayer
And supplication oft.
At last one died but Dan was calm,
He hardly seemed to care;
He knelt beside the bullock's corpse
And offered up a prayer.

'One bullock Thou hast taken, Lord,
And so it seemeth best,
Thy will be done, but see my need
And spare to me the rest.'

A month went by. Dan's bullocks now
Were dying every day,
But still on each occasion would
The faithful fellow pray,
'Another Thou hast taken, Lord,
And so it seemeth best,
Thy will be done, but see my need,
And spare to me the rest!'

And still they camped beside the hole,
And still it never rained,
And still Dan's Bullocks died and died,
Till only one remained.
Then Dan broke down – good Holy Dan –
The man who never swore.
He knelt beside the latest corpse
And here's the prayer he prore.

'That's nineteen Thou hast taken, Lord,
And now You'll plainly see
You'd better take the bloody lot,
One's no damn good to me.'
The other riders laughed so much
They shook the sky around;
The lightning flashed, the thunder roared,
And Holy Dan was drowned.

Anonymous

Paroo River

It was a week from Christmas-time,
As near as I remember,
And half a year since, in the rear,
We'd left the Darling timber.
The track was hot and more than drear;
The day dragged out forever;
But now we knew that we were near
Our camp – the Paroo River.

With blighted eyes and blistered feet,
With stomachs out of order,
Half-mad with flies and dust and heat
We'd crossed the Queensland border.
I longed to hear a stream go by
And see the circles quiver;
I longed to lay me down and die
That night on Paroo River.

The 'nose-bags' heavy on each chest
(God Bless one kindly squatter),
With grateful weight our hearts they pressed –
We only wanted water.
The sun was setting in a spray
Of colour like a liver –
We fondly hoped to camp and stay
That night by Paroo River.

A cloud was on my mate's broad brow,

And once I heard him mutter;
'What price the good old Darling now?
God bless that grand old gutter!'
And then he stopped and slowly said
In tones that made me shiver:
'It cannot well be on ahead –
I think we've crossed the river.'

But soon we saw a strip of ground
Beside the track we followed,
No damper than the surface round
But just a little hollowed.
His brow assumed a thoughtful frown –
This speech he did deliver:
'I wonder if we'd best go down
Or up the blessed river?'

'But where,' said I 'Is the blooming stream?'
And he replied, 'We're at it!'
I stood a while, as in a dream,
'Great Scot!' I cried, 'is that it?'
Why, that is some old bridle-track!;
He chuckled, 'Well, I never!
It's plain you've never been Out Back –
This is the Paroo River!'

Henry Lawson, 1867-1922

Down the River

Hark, the sound of it drawing nearer,
Clink of hobble and brazen bell;
Mark the passage of stalwart shearer,
Bidding Monaro soil farewell.
Where is he making for? Down the river,
Down the river to seek a 'shed'.

Where is his dwelling on old Monaro?
Buckley's Crossing, or Jindaboine?
Dry Plain, is it, or sweet Bolaira?
P'raps 'tis near where the rivers join.
Where is he making for? Down the river,
When, oh when, will he turn him back?
Soft sighs follow him down the river,
Moist eyes gaze at his fading track.

See, behind him his pack-horse, ambling,
Bears the weight of his master's kit,
Oft and oft from the pathway rambling,
Crops unhampered by cruel bit.
Where is he making for? Equine rover,
Sturdy nag from the Eucumbene,
Tempted down by the thought of clover,
Springing luscious in the Riverine.

Dreams of life and its future chances,
Snatch of song to beguile the way;
Through green crannies the sunlight glances,

Silver-gilding the bright 'Jack Shay'.
'So long, mate, I can stay no longer,
So long, mate, I've no time to stop;
Pens are waiting me at Mahonga,
Bluegong, Grubben and Pullitop.

'What! You say that the river's risen?
What! That the melted snow has come?
What! That it locks and bars our prison?
Many's the mountain stream I've swum.
I must onward and cross the river,
So long, mate, for I cannot stay;
I must onward and cross the river,
Over the river there lies my way.'

One man short when the roll they're calling,
One man short at old Bobby Rand's;
Heads are drooping and tears are falling
Up on Monaro's mountain lands.
Where is he making for? Down the river,
Down the river of slimy bed;
Where is he making for? Down the river,
Down the river that bears him, dead.

Barcroft Boake, 1866-1892

The Horse in the Tree

High in the fork of a gnarled old tree
Was the skeleton of a horse
By the road that wandered to Wirrandee;
And I said to Charlie, who rode with me,
'Left there by a flood, of course.'

But Charlie answered, 'Well I must say
You fellows make me smile;
For every person that comes this way
Just thinks the same, an' he's miles astray.
Now, I'll give you the dinkum ile.

'I was on that moke when he stuck up there –
'Twas a wonder I wasn't killed;
But seein' impediments everywhere
I shifted back in the atmosphere
An' only got bumped and spilled.

'You see, I was after a brumby mob,
Which hereabouts split an' spread,
Goin' lickety-split, me an Wirrandee Bob,
An' didn't see, till I reached that knob,
The tangle o' scrub ahead.

'The only openin' was through that fork,
An' 'fore I had time to think,
Blue Streak went up like a popped-up cork,
But the game old moke was fat as pork
And jammed like a wedge in a chink.

'An' there's his bones; 'tis a wonder how
They've hung in the sun and shade;
But 'The Horse in the Tree' is a landmark now
That drovers know, an' they all allow
'Twas a dam' fine leap he made.'

Edward S. Sorenson, 1869-1940

Featherstonhaugh

Brookong station lay half asleep
Dozed in the waning western glare
('Twas before the run had been stocked with sheep
And only cattle depastured there)
As the Bluecap mob reined up at the door
And loudly saluted Featherstonhaugh.

'My saintly preacher,' the leader cried,
'I stand no nonsense, as you're aware,
I've a word for you if you'll step outside,
Just drop that pistol and have a care;
I'll trouble you, too, for the key of the store,
For we're short of tucker, friend Featherstonhaugh.'

The muscular Christian showed no fear,
Though he handed the key, with but small delay;
He never answered the ruffian's jeer
Except by a look which seemed to say –

'Beware my friend, and think twice before
You raise the devil in Featherstonhaugh . . .

Two hours after he reined his horse
Up in Urana, and straightaway went
To the barracks – the trooper was gone, of course,
Blindly nosing a week-old scent
Away in the scrub around Mount Galore.
'Confound the fellow!' quoth Featherstonhaugh.

'Will any man of you come with me
And give this Bluecap a dressing-down?'
They all regarded him silently
As he turned his horse, with a scornful frown,
'You're curs, the lot of you, to the core –
I'll go by myself,' said Featherstonhaugh.

The scrub was thick on Urangeline
As he followed the tracks that twisted through
The box and dogwood and scented pine
(One of their horses had cast a shoe).
Steeped from his youth in forest lore
He could track like a black, could Featherstonhaugh.

He paused as he saw the thread of smoke
From the outlaw camp, and he marked the sound
Of a hobble check, as it sharply broke
The silence that held the scrub-land bound.
There were their horses – two, three, four –
'It's a risk, but I'll chance it!' quoth Featherstonhaugh.

He loosed the first, and it walked away,

But his comrade's silence could not be bought,
For he raised his head with a sudden neigh,
And plainly showed that he'd not be caught.
As a bullet sang from a rifle-bore –
'It's time to be moving,' quoth Featherstonhaugh.

The brittle pine, as they broke away,
Crackled like ice in a winter's ponds,
The strokes fell fast on the cones that lay
Buried beneath the withered fronds
That softly carpet the sandy floor –
Swept two on the tracks of Featherstonhaugh.

They struck the path that the stock had made,
A dustily-red, well-beaten track,
The leader opened a fusillade
Whose target was Featherston's stooping back
But his luck was out, not a bullet tore
As much as a shred from Featherstonhaugh.

Rattle 'em, rattle 'em fast on the pad,
Where the sloping shades fell dusk and dim;
The manager's heart beat high and glad
For he knew the creek was a mighty swim,
Already he heard a smothered roar –
'They're done like a dinner!' quoth Featherstonhaugh.

It was almost dark as they neared the dam;
He struck the crossing as true as a hair:
For the space of a second the pony swam,
Then shook himself in the chill night air.
In a pine-tree shade on the further shore,

With his pistol cocked, stood Featherstonhaugh.

A splash – an oath –a rearing horse,
A thread snapped short in the fateful loom,
The tide, unaltered, swept on its course
Though a fellow creature had met his doom:
Pale and trembling, and struck with awe,
Bluecap stood opposite Featherstonhaugh.

While the creek rolled muddily in between
The eddies played with the drowned man's hat.
The stars peeped out in the summer sheen,
A night-bird chirruped across the flat –
Quoth Bluecap, 'I owe you a heavy score,
And I'll live to repay it, Featherstonhaugh.'

But he never did, for he ran his race
Before he had time to fulful his oath.
I can't think how, but, in any case,
He was hung, or drowned, or maybe both.
Whichever it was, he came no more
To trouble the peace of Featherstonhaugh.

Barcroft Boake, 1866-1892

Mad Jack's Cockatoo

There was a man that went out in the floodtime
  and drought,
By the banks of the outer Barcoo,
And they called him Mad Jack 'cause the swag
  on his back
Was the perch of an old cockatoo.

By the towns near and far, in shed, shanty and bar
Came the yarns of Mad Jack and his bird,
And this tale I relate (it was told by a mate)
Is just one of the many I've heard.

Now Jack was a bloke who could drink, holy smoke,
He could swig twenty mugs to my ten,
And that old cockatoo, it could sink quite a few,
And it drank with the rest of the men.

One day when the heat was a thing hard to beat,
Mad Jack and his old cockatoo
Came in from the West – at the old Swagman's Rest.
Jack ordered the schooners for two.

And when these had gone down he forked out half
  a crown,
And they drank till the money was spent,
Then Jack pulled out a note from his tattered old
  coat
And between them they drank every cent.

Then that old cockatoo, it swore red, black and blue,
And it knocked all the mugs off the bar,
Then it flew through the air, and it pulled at the hair
Of a bloke who was drinking Three Star.

And it jerked out the pegs from the barrels and kegs,
Knocked the bottles all down from the shelf,
With a sound like a cheer it dived into the beer,
And it finished up drowning itself.

When at last Mad Jack woke from his sleep he ne'er
spoke,
But he cried like a lost husband's wife,
And each quick falling tear made a flood with the
beer,
And the men had to swim for their life.

Then Mad Jack he did drown; when the waters
went down
He was lying there stiffened and blue,
And it's told far and wide that stretched out by his
side
Was his track mate — the old cockatoo.

Anonymous

A Bushman's Song

I'm travellin' down the Castlereagh,
And I'm a station-hand,
I'm handy with the ropin' pole,
I'm handy with the brand,
And I can ride a rowdy colt,
Or swing the axe all day,
But there's no demand for a station-hand
Along the Castlereagh.

So it's shift, boys, shift,
For there isn't the slightest doubt
That we've got to make a shift
To the stations further out,
With the packhorse runnin' after,
For he follows like a dog,
We must strike across the country
At the old jig-jog.

This old black horse I'm riding –
If you'll notice what's his brand,
He wears a crooked R, you see –
None better in the land.
He takes a lot of beatin',
And the other day we tried,
For a bit of a joke, with a racing bloke,
For twenty pounds a side.

It was shift, boys, shift,
For there wasn't the slightest doubt

That I had to make him shift,
For the money was further out;
But he cantered home a winner,
With the other one at the flog –
He's a red-hot sort to pick
With his old jig-jog.

I asked a cove for shearin' once
Along the Matthaguy:
We shear non-union here,' says he
'I call it scab,' says I.
I looked along the shearin' floor
Before I turned to go –
There were eight or ten non-union men
A-shearin' in a row.

It was shift, boys, shift,
For there wasn't the slightest doubt
It was time to make a shift
With the leprosy about.
So I saddled up my horse,
And I whistled to my dog,
And I left his scabby station
At the old jig-jog.

I went to Illawarra,
Where my brother's got a farm;
He has to ask his landlord's leave
Before he lifts his arm;
The landlord owns the countryside –
Man, woman, dog and cat,

They haven't the cheek to dare to speak
Without they touch their hat.

It was shift, boys, shift,
For there wasn't the slightest doubt
Their little landlord god and I
Would soon be falling out;
Was I to touch my hat to him? –
Was I his bloomin' dog?
So I makes for up the country
At the old jig-jog.

But it's time that I was movin',
I've a mighty way to go
Till I drink artesian water
From a thousand feet below;
Till I meet the overlanders
With the cattle coming down –
And I'll work a while till I makes a pile,
Then have a spree in town.

So it's shift, boys, shift,
For there isn't the slightest doubt
We've got to make a shift
To the stations further out;
The packhorse runs behind us,
For he follows like a dog,
And we cross a lot of country
At the old jig-jog.

A.B. ('Banjo') Paterson, 1864-1941

The Fire at Thompson's Ford

Hottest of hot December days,
Fierce and strong are the sun's keen rays,
The north wind's sulphurous breath blows strong;
Even the magpie stills his song.
Over the pools of the stagnant creek
Steaming hangs the vaporous reek.
Under the scanty she-oaks crowd
Panting cattle, breathing loud.

Slowly, out in the eastern sky,
A wreath of smoke climbs clear and high,
It sways in the air like a tangled cord –
A fire has started at Thompson's ford!

Thompson's shed is late this year,
Most of his sheep are yet to shear;
'Blackleg' labour, with half a board –
No 'truck' with the union at Thompson's ford.
The union camp breaks up today;
Horses are saddled and ready, but stay!
Thompson shears with the 'scabs'. Just so,
But a big bushfire is a common foe.

Down the gully, along the flat,
Red Bill leading with one-eyed Mat;
Past the stockyard, over the brush,
Mat now first, the rest in a crush;
Seven long miles in a blazing sun,

And yet the prelude has but begun.

The flames in mountains roar and swirl;
Dense black smoke-clouds over them curl;
Bounding, crackling, leaping higher –
Ah, strong men shrink from a big bushfire!
'A real old bender,' says Mat, 'good Lord!
But we've got to stop at Thompson's ford.'
The river at Thompson's ford runs low –
'But the homestead goes if it's crossed, you know.'

Yes, that was a battle, and, even now,
The very thought just pains my brow.
Choked with smoke, dry as a board,
With our teeth hard-set we hold the ford.
Side by side in that desperate band,
Squatter and shearer, hand to hand,
Fought like tigers for hour on hour,
Never a man was seen to cower.
The sun in the west began to sink,
When, choking, panting, gasping for drink,
We sent up a cheer, aye, how we roared –
We had stopped the fire at Thompson's ford!

Next year, Thompson's notice states:
'Shearers wanted, union rates.'

'Womba'

The Man Who Came to Burrambeit

His eyes were blue, his skin was white,
Though tanned his face to cruel brown,
He seemed so weak and limp and light
As from the coach they passed him down –
In short, he seemed in woeful plight
The man who came to Burrambeit.

The driver gravely shook his head,
'The pore young cove is green yer know,
I've 'eard 'im wish that 'e was dead
The 'orrid sun did try 'im so!
'Is parents they ain't done wot's right
In sending 'im to Burrambeit!'

For three whole days the stranger lay,
Within the pub shut out from view;
He'd sent a little note to say
The bush was all so strange and new,
He hoped that they'd forgive his plight,
The kindly folk of Burrumbeit.

And when at last quite pale and thin
The stranger showed upon the scene,
The good folk rushed to take him in
He seemed so very young and green –
To put the poor young stranger right,
Stirred every heart in Burrambeit.

He told them he had come from town

His parents – both alas! – were dead,
But he would live his troubles down
In spite of hot suns overhead;
In fact, he'd work with all his might
And win the praise of Burrambeit.

The kindly folk gave ear with pride
To all the stranger had to say,
It is a noble thing they cried,
That man should act in such a way;
In spite of luck to make a fight
Appeals to us at Burrambeit!

They made him welcome to each home,
They tended him with eager zest,
They told him he was free to roam
Just as his fancy pleased him best,
In short, they made a hero quite
Of that young man in Burrambeit.

And when the races came, they cried,
'Now to the meeting you must go,
There's no place round the countryside
Can show the sport that we can show!
The best of owners we invite
To send their gees to Burrambeit!'

The young man laughed, and cried, 'What fun!
Oh! shan't I love to see the course;
But I shall bet before I'm done,
I know I shall, upon some horse!'
His eagerness reached such a height

It made them laugh at Burrambeit.

But fate, alas! proved most unkind
Fore ere the third race had begun,
The young man soon began to find
He could not bear the blazin' sun.
'Dear friends,' he cried, 'It's hopeless quite,
I must return to Burrambeit!'

With faltering step he turned away
A teardrop gleaming in his eye,
'Oh! what would I not give to stay,'
He quavered as he waved good-bye;
'But never mind, I'll soon be right;
Don't grieve, dear friends of Burrambeit!'

Then climbing sadly on his horse
He slowly turned and rode away,
But when some distance from the course
His manner changed, I'm bound to say,
For suddenly with all his might
He galloped back to Burrambeit!

He rode until he came to where
The bank lay sleeping in the sun;
One youthful clerk alone was there,
For there was nothing to be done –
To hope for work, was useless quite
With races on at Burrambeit!

The stranger raised his hat of felt
As quietly he entered there;

Then taking something from his belt
He waved it gently in the air;
The clerk turned pink, and green, and white
For he was new to Burrambeit!

'Young man,' the stranger softly said,
'You're here alone, as I've been told,
So if you'd rather not be dead
Just hand me out your stocks of gold;
Your movements, too, pray expedite,
I think of leaving Burrambeit.'

The clerk, all trembling, turned away
And did as he was told, of course;
And all the gold, I'm grieved to say,
Was soon upon the stranger's horse;
The poor young cove who felt the sun!
But death seemed sad at Burrambeit.

The stranger once more softly cried,
'I hate to be an awful bore,
But I'm afraid you must be tied
With rope, and left upon the floor;
To find you in this sorry plight
Will soothe the wrath of Burrumbeit.'

The stranger laughed, as like a pig,
He rolled the clerk upon the floor,
Then, taking off his auburn wig,
He pinned in gaily to the door,
And underneath these words did write:
'A keepsake for dear Burrambeit!'

And this is true without a doubt
That, if you're anxious for some fun,
Just tell those gentle folk about
The poor young cove who felt the sun!
You'll find they've not forgotten quite.
And you'll remember Burrambeit!

R. Allen ('Guy Eden')

A Yarn of Lambing Flat

'Call that a yarn!' said old Tom Pugh,
'What rot! I'll lay my hat
I'll sling a yarn worth more nor two
Such pumped up yarns as that.'
And thereupon old Tommy 'slew'
A yarn of Lambing Flat.

'When Lambing Flat broke out,' he said,
' 'Mongst others there I know
A lanky, orkard, Lunnon-bred
Young chap named Johnnie Drew,
And nicknamed for his love of bed,
The Sleeping Beauty too.

'He sunk a duffer on the Flat
In comp'ny with three more,
And makin' room for this and that

They was a tidy four,
Save when the eldest, Dublin Pat,
Got drunk and raved for gore.

'This Jack at yarnin' licked a book,
And half the night he'd spout,
But when he once turn'd in, it took
Old Nick to get him out.
And that is how they came to cook
The joke I tell about.

'A duffer-rush broke out one day,
I quite forget where at –
(It doesn't matter, anyway,
It didn't feed a cat) –
And Johnnie's party said they'd say
Good-bye to Lambing Flat.

'Next morn rose Johnnie's mates to pack
And make an early shunt,
But all they could get out of Jack
Was 'All right', or a grunt,
By pourin' water down his back
And – when he turned – his front.

'The billy boiled, the tea was made,
They sat and ate their fill,
But Jack, upon his broad back laid,
Snored like a foghorn still;
"We'll save some tea to scald him," said
The peaceful Corney Bill.

'As they their beef and damper ate
And swilled their pints of tea
A bully notion all at wonst
Dawned on that roudy three.
And Dublin Pat, in frantic mirth,
Said, "Now we'll have a spree!"

'Well, arter that, I'm safe to swear,
The beggars didn't lag,
But packed their togs with haste and care,
And each one made his swag
With Johnnie's moleskins, every pair
Included in the bag.

'With nimble fingers from the pegs
They soon the string unbent,
And off its frame as sure as eggs
They drew the blessed tent,
And rolled it up and stretched their legs,
And packed the lot – and went.

'And scarcely p'raps a thing to love,
The 'Beauty' slumbered sound,
With nought but heaven's blue above
And Lambing Flat around,
Until in sight some diggers hove –
Some diggers out'ard bound.

'They sez as twelve o'clock was nigh –
We'll say for sure eleven –
When Johnnie ope'd his right-hand eye
And looked straight up to heaven:

I reckon he got more surprise
Than struck the fabled Seven.

'Clean off his bunk he made a bound,
And when he rubbed his eyes
I'm safe to swear poor Johnnie found
His dander 'gin to rise.
For there were diggers standin' round –
Their missuses likewise.

'Oh, Lor'! the joke – it warn't lost,
Though it did well nigh tear
The sides of them as came acrost
The flat to hear Jack swear.
They sez as how old Grimshaw tossed
His grey wig in the air.

'Some minutes on the ground Jack lay,
And bore their screamin' jeers,
And every bloke that passed that way
Contributed his sneers:
Jack groaned aloud, that cursed day
Seemed lengthened into years.

'Then in a fury up he sprung –
A pretty sight, you bet –
And laid about him with his tongue
Advising us to 'get'.
And praying we might all be hung
I think I hear him yet.

'Then, on a sudden, down he bent,

And grabbed a chunk of rock,
And into Grimshaw's stomach sent
The fossil, with a shock,
And Grimshaw doubled up and went
To pieces with the knock.

'And in the sun that day Jack stood
Clad only in his shirt,
And fired with stones and bits of wood,
And with his tongue threw dirt,
He fought as long as e'er he could –
But very few were hurt.

'He stooped to tear a lump of schist
Out of the clinging soil,
By thunder you should heard him jist,
And seen the way he'd coil
Upon the ground, and hug his fist,
And scratch and dig and toil!

' 'Twas very plain he'd struck it fat,
The dufferin' Lunnon Muff:
The scoff and butt of Lambing Flat
Who always got it rough,
Could strike his fortune where he sat:
The joker held the stuff.

'Well, that's the yarn, it ain't so poor:
Them golden days is o'er,
And Dublin Pat was drowned, and sure
It quenched his thirst for gore;
Old Corney Bill and Dave the Cure

I never heard no more.

'The Sleepin' Beauty's wealthy, too,
And wears a shiny hat,
But often comes to old Tom Pugh
To have a quiet chat:
I lent him pants to get him through
His fix on Lambing Flat.

Anonymous

Waltzing Matilda

Once a jolly swagman camped by a billabong
Under the shade of a coolibah tree,
And he sang as he watched
And waited till his billy boiled,
'Who'll come a-waltzing Matilda with me?
Waltzing Matilda, waltzing Matilda,
Who'll come a-waltzing Matilda with me?'
And he sang as he watched
And waited till his billy boiled,
'Who'll come a-waltzing Matilda with me?'

Down came a jumbuck to drink at that billabong;
Up jumped the swagman and grabbed him with glee.
And he sang as he shoved that jumbuck
In his tucker-bag,

'You'll come a-waltzing Matilda with me.
Waltzing Matlida, waltzing Matilda,
You'll come a-waltzing Matilda with me.'
And he sang as he shoved that jumbuck
In his tucker-bag,
'You'll come a-waltzing Matilda with me.'

Up rode the squatter, mounted on his thoroughbred;
Down came the troopers, one, two, three:
'Whose' that jolly jumbuck
You've got in your tucker-bag?
You'll come a-waltzing Matilda with me!'

Up jumped the swagman and sprang into
  the billabong:
'You'll never catch me alive!' said he;
And his ghost may be heard as you pass by
  that billabong,
'You'll come a-waltzing Matilda with me!
Waltzing Matilda, waltzing Matilda,
You'll come a-waltzing Matilda with me!'
And his ghost may be heard
As you pass by that billabong'
You'll come a-waltzing Matilda with me!'

A.B. ('Banjo') Paterson, 1864-1941

Index of Titles

Index of First Lines

Acknowledgement

'My Country' has been reproduced with the
permission of the copyright owners: the Estate
of Dorothea Mackellar, A. Coffison and S. Kruger,
care of Curtis Brown (Australia).

The Five Mile Press Pty Ltd
22 Summit Road
Noble Park Victoria 3174
Australia

Published in 2001
This compilation © The Five Mile Press Pty Ltd
Editor: Maggie Pinkney
Designer: Geoff Hocking

Printed in Australia by Griffin Press
National Library of Australia
Cataloguing-in-Publication data
Classic Australian verse
Includes index.
ISBN 1 86503 491 6.
1. Australian poetry. 2. Ballads, English - Australia
3. Folk songs, English – Australia. I. Pinkney, Maggie
A821.008

Cover Image:
Tom Roberts
Bailed Up, 1895/1927
Oil on canvas, 134.5 x 182.8 cm
Art Gallery of New South Wales
Photograph: Ray Woodbury for AGNSW